He jerked it into the boat
and slit the belly open :
lists, inventories,
mouths pressed between pages,
ancient cities half digested,
and all the lost languages vanishing once more
into the skin
like colors that are only true in darkness.

Berkeley Poets Cooperative
Anthology 1970–1980

Production by JoAnn Ugolini, Dorothy Wall
Frontispiece poem by Bruce Hawkins
Cover by Anthony Dubovsky

Our thanks to the California Arts Council, the National Endowment for the Arts and
the Coordinating Council of Literary Magazines for their continued support.

Special thanks to the West Coast Print Center for their excellent work and assistance
over the years and to Ramsay Bell for her generous contribution.

ISBN 0-917658-12-4

Typeset by M. A. Hayden at the West Coast Print Center, Berkeley, California

Preface

The Berkeley Poets' Cooperative is a nonprofit organization which offers writers the opportunity to explore, develop and publish their works. We are the oldest such organization in the country. Our first magazine appeared in 1970. Our chapbook series began in 1974. For more than a decade we have maintained a free public workshop in poetry and fiction. The small press world has always been one of high infant mortality : the average magazine survives less than a year, less than two issues. We believe our relative longevity can be credited to openness, flexibility and our strong identification with the Berkeley community.

For many local writers our workshops provide the chance to receive reaction and criticism from other individuals committed to the same craft as themselves. Meetings range in size from 10 to 35 participants; more than 100 writers will attend in the course of a year. Our magazine presents the best material from the workshop along with submissions received through the mail. To avoid clique publishing, editorial staffs rotate constantly. Talented writers and artists who are willing to contribute energy can rise quickly to positions of authority in the Co-op structure. And we remain the only writers' cooperative to consider and publish books by nonmembers.

The volume you are now holding is our first anthology. We have tried to be as eclectic as possible. Every writer and work published by the Co-op was considered, and these final choices represent over nine months of meetings and discussions. Any "best of" collection intends quality. Inevitably, it must also involve taste and politics. The staff wrestled with such issues in the course of the selection process. In many cases, it is clear, different staffs would have made different choices. Yet throughout the process we feel that our major aim remained intact: to put together a collection which reflects the spectrum of writing talent which the Berkeley Poets' Cooperative has attracted and nurtured over the years.

Contents

Introduction

"Poetry fettered fetters the human race." William Blake said that and I believe it. Blake would have approved of the San Francisco Bay Area Renaissance, which released poetry from the smooth hands of the academics, and returned it to our lives.

It was the rainy spring of 1973 when I first meandered into the Berkeley Poets' Co-op. I was on sabbatical, working on notes to Blake's poems and working on my own poems, with my husband, who is an astrophysicist, and I had met some fine astrophysicists at Berkeley but no poets. It was lonely. But these people were supposed to be meeting Wednesday nights at Charles and Maggie Entrekin's on Oregon Street. When I biked over, I felt shy. I could see them through the porch windows before I came in. They were so young, they were sitting packed on the floor, they radiated intensity in waves through the windows.

Everyone knows poets are mad exhibitionists. We feel so all alone when we write. Non-poets don't understand us, we think. And we want to shine. We want the people to say to us: hey, that's great, what a great poem. But more than that, if we are serious, we need to spend time in a world where people care about writing, know how important it is.

BPC was the best workshop I'd ever belonged to. Anybody could walk in off the streets with a poem, and read it there: teenage runaways and bearded seers down from the commune in the mountains, not-so-gay divorcees, students fresh from Eng. Lit. 451, computer engineers, auto mechanics. No authority figure ran the show. Charles might shift us along when we repeated ourselves. Bruce would be silent for an hour then come around the corner like a fast truck. I had been in groups where the object was to drop people's poems into a shredder—some set of *a priori* correct poetic principles—and watch them disintegrate. I'd been in workshops where the object was mutual ego stroking. BPC was not a therapy group. Yet there was always the understanding that poetry is our lives, there on a limb, putting out leaves in the dangerous air. We were writing about what mattered to us, and each of us had to respect that in the others. So if a naive young creature read a poem about the vastness of the universe, and thought he invented the subject, I had to pay attention. If a woman read about some man hurting her, the men listened.

People can attend the Co-op for a while and drift off. They have (everyone has!)

one or two poems curled in them like embryos. The group becomes their midwife, and they have these poems forever.

The permanently committed writers of prose and poetry in BPC, who cared over the long haul about human emotions and right language, and were working to marry them, kept coming back. They paid sustained attention to each other's lives, feelings, words. They fought each other from time to time. "Opposition is true friendship," Blake says. The meetings kept on and the best work continued sifting into issues of the BPC magazine, which began to appear in 1970 and is now the oldest surviving co-op magazine in the country. The magazine's editions of 3000 copies sell out, largely through street sales, thanks to the genius of Bruce Hawkins, who can spot a secret poetry lover a block away down Telegraph, thanks to the excellence of the work the magazine prints, which finds its own audience. In 1974 BPC began its chapbook series. The best work from the magazine and the chapbooks is collected in this anthology.

Before I left Berkeley we helped collate an issue of the magazine. It was a good party. Back East, I helped start US1 Poets' Co-op because I missed BPC. I explain today that the poetry scene in the Bay Area is the most vital in the country. That is something that did not die with the sixties. It is neither commercial nor academic. It is Charles knowing how love pulls and tears at us, love of men and women, parents and children, wilderness outside and inside. It is Bruce creating a nursing home where

> the world's a
> mean place, meaner than those fans
> in the outfield in Detroit.
> It takes a man like Pepper
> Martin to face up to it . . .
> . . . . .
> they have a new trick now,
> they splash water in his face
> until it feels like he is crying.

It is the funny prose fantasies of Kit Duane and Paul Bendix, and Lucy Day urging her daughter toward sexuality. It is Pat Dienstfrey watching a neighbor boy who cannot talk to people:

> But when he calls his cat at midnight
> his voice is clear,
> goes easily over the garden
> as if the world were empty.

There is happiness and grief in this anthology. Politics and personal experience. Renaissance means rebirth, and the anthology shows that rebirth is still happening.

Alicia Ostriker
Rutgers University

Dedicated to the people of Berkeley whose support made these ten years possible.

Karen Brodine

THERE IS A REFUSAL TO BE DROWNED

that floats my breasts up plump
in the tub   that wants the fat moon
to tongue the uncurtained glass
that lets my hands find you and continue
to want   there is a refusal
to be drowned   that buoys me up
from a silent man to tread water
toward you   how many times
have we talked until light   if we shape
poems   discarding a sock   a blouse   a bad
line   a shoe   how long till we lie
unnightgowned together speaking
in tongues

YOU ASK ME TO SAY

you ask me to say how I care for you
how you change me

a hand reaches out of my mouth and snaps it shut

we are closed.   our eyes stare out
like distant cousins.

we know this flat look of hurt
the hard plateau that jars the knees, the chest.

and if you, warm in the morning,
speak to me in your tousled voice,
this does not change me ?

or when I am witch, driven to wall, screaming
alone   alone   alone
this is not indifference.

finding a balance is trying to stop
the fig trees in our yard from their restless swaying
or trying to set them moving on a still day.

THEY HAVE DRESSED
AND UNCLOTHED TWICE

eating artichokes
they discuss the soul.
"this separation of spirit
from flesh?" she asks,
pulling off a tender
leaf, dipping it.
he disagrees, pulling
ahead to the heart.
she assumes—no soul,
he hopes for one.
a few leaves plunk
to the floor.

   . . .

looking out the window of the room
where they have spent hours
trying to agree,
she says, "look at the snow—
thistles fill the air.
the trees are trimmed with feathers
and strange birds,
ruffled and white,
graze on the crops.
just as he glances out,
her vision disappears.
he sees a few thistles drift by.

   . . .

they have dressed and unclothed twice.
she pulls his shirt
over his shoulders,
buttons it.
the white buttons grin.
she draws his jeans
up his white legs, his hips,
closes the zipper.
last she tilts his hat
so it shadows his face.
he reaches for her in slow motion
draws her blouse
around her shoulders.

HENS

Hens, the dark red flock
thrown out against the snow
like drops of blood.

An old woman in black
shoos them to the roadside
where they cackle, soft and plump.

I stagger by on the ice, as usual.
Snap, snap, the hens clack
their beaks, swallowing air.
I stumble and they ruffle
clipped wings.

My friend and I try
to hold each other up
on the ice,
take time to be gentle,
solemnly trading coats.
For we must escape
in opposite directions.

I tell her a story before we leave.
Of the straggly thin-necked ones.
They have no sense.
When the uncommon snow softens our fields
they lose all sense of direction,
wander out to settle on snow-nests
hunch there still
pin-feathered islands.

Their eyes, wide-open and unsurprised,
absorb the white of the white field.

I am the home person, the one who sits in a room at a desk
the one who kneads bread and rises

I am the homed pigeon who ruffles her feathers, expectant
of a message to land on her shoulder
who wraps the bright foil of a sentence around her wrist
then wonders where to deliver it

Sometimes I spend all day walking from room to room, looking out
Sometimes I lean on the walls and they soften to cloth
and I pull them over my head and dream

I watch the yard carefully for signs
The trees each day slip a little more out
of their leaves so I see
the neighborhood clearer and clearer

I am liable to be home even now drinking tea
keeping the kitchen warm with all the burners on
trying to tell exactly how the light at evening eases away

THE HOUSE IS ALIVE,
THE SNOW IS BURNING

This bright cell of a honey comb
the wood translucent after long exposure to heat
ribs of paper lampshade glowing

The eyelid is the eye's red tent
each day my body eats the light
and gives back fever

In this room that holds itself together by light
I am wanting to fly apart in crystals
the way snow falls upward in a good storm

My books, plates, shoes, hang on the porch
clanging and swinging in the wind
let them fly off that rope and roll into the dark

Taste the salt and ash of the drifting house
touch the knots, the knuckle bones, the red
roses simmering in a bowl.

THE MARE IS DROWNING

She slips and plunges into the well.
The water displaced by her weight
rushes over our feet. She sinks,
eyes closed, pale mane drifting up
like sea grass. We grab her mane,
drag her up, tilt her head so air rushes

into her mouth as water streams out.
It takes all our strength to let her
down into the water, drag her up,
down and up—till she gulps, shudders,
and like a great hummingbird, pulls us
with her. Our feet skim the ground.
She is breathing on her own
with a rough, deep sound.

WHAT SHE DID IN MY DREAM

The reason the dream keeps coming back is it keeps
being true. The branch keeps springing into my face
because it is the same path. This time I see the woman
has a wide brow and grey eyes. She tells me to walk
up that path and write how it is to be a woman
who has decided to have no children. Dusk evens out
the sharp brambles. As I climb it easily darkens
to full night. I hear the faint joyful voices of children
that run past me down the path. I come to a structure
built of sweetsmelling new wood, climb the ramp,
switch on a light bulb. Seeing how bare and empty it is,
I think, "but this will be a good place to work."

Dan Balderston

MURDEROUS SESTINA

(for someone who had best remain nameless
with thanks to my teacher thom gunn)

this isn't the first time i've thought of killing you
the last few months often in the middle of the night
as i lay cursing that sleep wouldn't come to bed
i wondered unknown to my parents and neighbors
how it would feel that act of killing
and what to use knife razorblade or gun

except for the expense and inexperience the gun
has obvious advantages in that with it you
would have less chance of surviving the killing
which would come unexpected some chance night
when two or three shots would awaken the neighbors
and they'd find us lying for love on the bed

for love o what fantasies i have of that bed
i barely remember it (o yes thomson gunn
this writing is vivid) i never met your neighbors
when i lent john the tent so he & your lover & you
could go camping i should have poisoned your night
like medea or herakles' wife—what a killing!

another scenario i have of the killing
while lying and thinking alone in my bed
is of driving across town some spring night
you don't lock your door—entering with gun
in hand turning on the light the two of you
would be dead before the neighbors

knew but that is a problem about the neighbors
because of them i'd doubtless end up killing
myself unfortunate yes but joining you
mixing our blood there on the bed
would be just in its way why then the gun
why need i get desperate again tonight?

that the remedies i contemplate often at night
are unnecessary you and your neighbors
may care to discuss before i bring my gun

kind of me isn't it to warn before killing
in a poem so lovely & orderly read it in bed
poetry all to delight and instruct you

if you have time the night of the killing
don't think of the neighbors asleep each in bed
but bless the gun by whose grace i wed you

FOR EUGENIA, WHO LOVES THISTLES

The weeds are growing out of my idleness.
Foxtails by the willow, other grasses
Other places, tough-stemmed vinca, dock
And dandelions, and thistles. Thistles, Eugenia!
Some too drab to mention, but, just below
The new magnolia and the native poppies,
A great leopard thistle, jagged leaves
Speckled with white, is bursting into bloom
To my shame; this poem may mark the end
Of its triumphant flowering, and my sloth.
Weeds, my botany professor says, grow,
Strangers, in waste and disturbed places.
Worse weeds are growing in the interior garden,
Poems worthier than that thistle of the hoe.

TO EMILY DICKINSON

The treefrogs are singing tonight, Emily,
Their song of the solitary heart. My own
Throbs quietly with them; it is oddly
Four years since I wrote them a poem.

I understand now why you chose to remain
A whole life in your father's house:
That the river of your sorrows might run
Always in a familiar bed; might wash

You nightly, that you might daily be
A new person, if always with wet feet.
You wrote most beautifully of the ecstasy
Of solitude—the freedom, the closeness to God—

But how many nights at your writing-table
Did you yearn to breathe, and felt unable?

Richard Marcus

OBITUARY
for Hart Crane

It wasn't the hootch
that killed him.
Nor even that wild horse
America,
panicking in her stall,
crushing a lot of other people
betweeen the wall and her brute ribs
But that
he tried to ride her!
   like a painting of the flying rails
He tried to ride her oiled back,   .
   like putting butter
   between the muscle and the wild meat
   to make those first days tender
   more tender than the snow;
the crumbling of lost and longing fingers . . .

He rode
   the settlers and their lame remnants
   into the roaring century,
   and ran the rumorous midnights
   down their tributaries
   following the epistles of the sea
   back to their source . . .

He found the animal
   larger than he thought,
   building in his thighs
   the same white heat
   which sluiced the molten rivers   ′
   from their ore,
   which let her cables twine
   in foundaries, braiding up her long wild hair.
   He found that heat soldered bodies to their fate,

And like the last, mad captain
Split so long by what he loved and hated
He rode her down
   unable and unwilling to escape
   Such things that called so deep,
so loud!

Laura Schiff

EASTER SUNDAY

Ladies of 1900 lounge above doorways
Atlas, Arpad, Zeus, or ersatz gods
all grow black with soot.
April is older.
The stores seem middle-aged with
plastic shoes and refrigerators.
Only the leaves ignore accumulation.
The beginning is always red-green, clean.
Along the Danube,
on benches in the sun
they are all asleep.
A fifty year old couple smile in their wedding bed,
they hold hands, eyes closed.
Three old ladies,
stick legs, cloche hat, ribbons of fur
sleep under dark sun glasses,
fox noses in the air.
A paunch sleeps.
Even the children play in slow motion.
I rush home to get a camera.
I'll snap death
that has relaxed and appeared,
but when I come back
they have all awakened.
A blind girl, like a squirrel scratching for acorns,
claws her book.
Death hides in her finger,
in a man peeling an orange,
in soft noises and small movements.

LULU

On a rain-cleared night, I'll leave my city
eager to tell her it looks like a forest of rhinestones.
I see things now, just to tell her.
I'll walk back to that dirt road
that row of shacks and houses
that stretch from islands of geese to cypresses

I'll walk past a muddy well
stray pea hens
ducks in ditches
a stiff bicycling peasant
locked in elbows with Lulu
my old gypsy
my story teller
my curled-up child
my soul
that pins a scrap of Botticelli
she found in a garbage pail onto her kitchen wall
my bawdy friend
I'll walk repeating her Hungarian lesson
"I wrenched my fart
you wrenched your fart
he wrenched his fart . . ."
and when she talks of neighbors and sons
and looks at the geranium skies and evening cows
and says "it's a good life, isn't it?"
I'll say "it is."

VELAZQUEZ

A room of white Marie-Thereses
in gold, orange, blue satin

Marie-Therese at 1 year, 2 years, 3, 4, 5, 6,
14 years, 21 years

And every morning Velazquez got up and started painting
a Marie-Therese.

And every morning we get up and do the same thing too
but sometimes for more than 21 years
sometimes less

and sometimes it doesn't grow ugly like the princess.

Nick Johnson

THEM
for my therapists

I know by their looks,
the way they carry themselves
like a burden,
eyes ringed like the moon.

I talk to them
like I talk to myself.
I tell them
I walk in the woods,

soundlessly,
like an Indian, setting
neat prints in the snow,
eyeing the squirrels.

I tell them that I sit
in the snow like a tree stump,
how my fingers and toes
drop off one by one,

how I count them as they drop.
My feelings fall off
like my clothes, silently,
snow closing my eyes.

I tell them
I have come here,
unwanted,
wished for like death,

that even the rabbit
gnaws off
its paw, rather than
be caught in a trap.

Edward Martinez

the bowl is filled with oatmeal;
my father is at work.
the trees are bare with winter
i see them naked—
like my father's lover in mexico,
but i cannot see the roots
buried beneath my vision.

in one hour, i will be off to school.
in two hours, my father will be home.
in six months, we will be in mexico
and i will ask to sleep in the car.
i will lock the doors to the world.
my father will sleep with a woman, worried.
i will close my eyes and feel the car moving.
my driver, just as my father, will remain unseen.

when i come home, my father will be sleeping
naked, exhausted, in his livingroom chair.
his penis will say to me—i am your father.
once at the age of nine, i slept soundly
between him and his lover
and his naked body sang to me—i am your father.
the song echoed from behind
thru the warmth of a foreign body.

at times he lives
deeper than breakfast or dinner
and the barmaids hover over him.
at times he dies and i exist
only as a parasite on my fathers death;
and the bull pasted on the pastel wall
is murdered by a lonely eye.

Charles Entrekin

HERE IN THE DARK, LOVE

I'm out here in the dark, love,
because I wanted to be alone.
Because I wanted something to give-in to.
I tried to remember how lives change, always
altered and yet remain the same, but tonight
    I felt something break
as after a long fall. Now even our names
seem best left alone, unchanged
like names buried character by character
in stone.
    I remember the tunes, love,
that's why I've come. I remember
the honeysuckle touch of your tongue.
    You can see I'm here without my clothes,
and the moon's not bright; but listen to me first,
something's gone wrong in my life, some
things I've not told you about. Listen.
Some blood always runs cold as mine.
This nakedness on the lawn
contains all I've ever been.
    I know you're going to say
I keep bringing you what has changed
without me.
    I know when I wake
in the morning my seed will remain
one more secret egg on your plate,
but you see I don't care, I also
will not know what's become of us.

BIRMINGHAM

Of all the places you could die
trapped if you didn't leave fast
or have lots of money, this is the one
you remember best. This is your birthplace.
    You wanted out the day she ran away,
left you the child and the furniture.
But you stayed, innocent and twenty-one,

made love to practiced women. One,
forty-one, who kept your child for free;
one, thirty-three, who hoped her husband
died, a little at a time; and one,
twenty-nine, who came to you animalized,
hardened with lies.

It was a steel time town, younger
and harder than Birmingham Sunday could break.
Three black children died. You made love
to the wife of a salesman. He failed
to give her children. And failed again
she cried when you stopped cold,
told her, no, no more children.

That night outside Memphis, the Mississippi
mosquitoes like furies bidding you goodbye,
you turn in your mind the meaning of escape.
Almost, you wanted to lie, you're innocent
if you don't go back. The child asleep, your red car
packed, you douse the fire and drive out fast.

HIGH, ALL NIGHT DRIVING TO BERKELEY

Drink beer, follow the headlights,
the highway knows where a woman waits
who loves me. Drunks pass on by;
all maniacs stay in bed; I'm high
and Berkeley's near with its strong
ocean-like ways. The desert behind, a song
plays in my ear. Already sea waves run white
lines one at a time down the moon-lit night.
Your tides pull me along; your curve of thigh
runs in my mind; your round brown eyes
close once again. Take me, take me, says the song;
the maps show I can make no wrong
decisions. Home, to know your body as before;
I am a desert, wrecked dreamer come to shore.

ADVANTAGE

In France beside some shabby old wall
the water runs dirty with sunlight
and I walk, moss-brown stones beneath my feet,

toward you with open arms.   You are blond now.
You have changed only the color of your hair.
All the rest remains the same.
        In your eyes I see you don't understand,
as if you're puzzled by my greeting.   Being polite
you invite me to coffee before finding you're afraid :
there are no witnesses.   Always we are alone.
It's then you begin to doubt, and I discover
once again how your grave face will unravel,
        remembering when we were young,
when your dark hair glistened like a river in the sun.

THE PHOTOGRAPH IS WRONG

        It was on a chert-red road near Birmingham,
our weathered gray farm house tilting
toward the earth. Green fingers of kudzu
had claimed the chimney and roof.
        When I look closely I can make out
railroad beds and a field of dead grass
in the distance. It was taken in Indian summer.
You are sitting under the mimosa trees, looking
like life had been good to you. It wasn't true.
        That was the year it snowed, a false spring
bloom on everything.   I remember pointing to the trees,
saying how beautiful they were, undressed that way
and standing in ice.

IN SAN FRANCISCO

Coming towards me
like light from a distant star
not yet arrived anywhere
he entered the park
fondling an animal-headed
smooth-carved redwood cane;
    then pushing his black
leather jacket loose at the neck
his dark-skinned hand
found and placed the harp,
the black eyes closing,
the coffined chords

a hymn, a dirge,
   and suddenly I know how
the sounds of what I have broken
are healing in the ground.

MISSOULA SPRING

   I have become
one of my own poems.
This morning the covered streets
opened black in melting snow.
   I was wrong.
Winter gone, a flower
opens in me, a song, words
crawl in my veins,
a carnation of the brain,
a dogwood.

ALABAMA KUDZU

This is the fear, the words
trapped in the back of your throat,
that nothing is enough.
   In your blood you trace
the inner latticework of kudzu,
you understand the brown trees,
all motion pulled to the ground,
like horses drowned in quicksand,
the tall and crumbling pine
beneath an undying green.
   But this is only the fear,
you have told yourself, regret nothing.
Your eyes are still blue, and inside
you are still capable of surrendering.

MASTERS

   I pick you out, a man to become,
yes and no together; you lead me
into the desert. Your single words
are too thick for meaning. I

can't make them out. The cactus
plants are all I understand. And
the heat.
    In the moment I take my eyes
away you fall in and die. Whose
death do I feel? This is all
a dream. I wake and think of
writing it down. A man walks
through my window from Montana.
"Thirty white geese are saved
from extinction," he says, and helps
himself to my liquor. We ignore
the snow.
    I was just in Mexico, I said,
and felt a man die. He rages out
in the midst of a blizzard, with my
liquor. This is another dream.
They flower like carnations in a bowl.
I am awake now. The white petals
fall away and sink.

THE ART OF POETRY

Once more, buddy, your last ride
has left you behind and nothing can be done.
You want someone to come, a silver angel,
to seize your hair and lift you from the earth.
    But the weight of your two feet
presses against the ground. No one comes
to save you. It's too cold to stand still
and too dark to run.
    Once more, buddy, you write
to save yourself. Here's the barn;
here the horses are warm; here, on a dark
night, between towns, between meals,
simply the heat of other animals is enough.

AWAKENING

I can hear the corners of my room touching,
The whole enclosed space leaning around and over me.
I am sealed inside, comfortable and warm, but

I have been out walking;
My hair is still damp with rain
And there is the feel of nearby fog
Moving around my feet.
My wool hat smells like a dead animal.

YES

We were waiting in a stand of pines. The hounds
announced themselves. Yes, he said, yes, they'll cross
over there. And he began to run.

I remember catching up, my uncle taking the pistol
from his clothes. He knelt by the road. It had rained
earlier that morning and the smoke stayed close to the
ground, the sound burning in my ears.

Yes, he said, fine rabbit if he doesn't have worms,
and he smiled, his hands disappearing once again beneath
his coat.

And the rabbit was so small, shot through the head,
I was amazed and puzzled, a child knowing that shot was
a feat of perfection somehow. So small and he had shot
it from so far away.

So small, and yes, he had stood there holding it
by the ears, the wind bending around us, the trees singing
the song of what could be remembered but never again touched.

EARTHSONG

And what could she say
who knew it best, took nothing
kept nothing and gave no warning
she would stop and turn away.

No one knows how it happens
these roads stretch out through
snow, flare, and turn to covered
hills, trees quiet as cows
gathered for night.

No insects hum. An old barn
cracks from the cold. Every night
her old body hides in the dark
under the rustle of corn leaves.

I want to reach out

pull the land away
reach down and hold her
shining like moon on the snow.

CRAZY LADY

Only dreams and sweet revenge from a soft
romance — someone stole her baby. Dilated
eyes now search your face. Was it you ?
A judge declared it best, and so look,
here's to elegance and extravagance
and her tough beauty on the streets.
        But today she's not high enough;
she feels the parenthesis of her sex
closing over emptiness. She moves
to hold you fast, poised at the edge
of herself. You have to make everything
simple, she says; align things by ones
before you divide.
        But touch no more than her
thin bare arms and a light
comes on inside her, and then a toast,
here's to her Byzantine beauty, and a home
away from home, sweet San Francisco,
here's to where she sleeps in the streets,
and her mouthtalker, eyeseer poetry.

PARTING

My father paced me as we shovelled
until I grew tired
and watched him
watching me
shovelling
and then when I stopped
he grinned
his feet sinking slowly in the loose dirt
the sweat pouring down his muscled back
in streams;
somehow he won then,
and even as I packed my bags
our angry eyes clashing like iron

and I turned my back on him
I felt that smile
as he shovelled on
past all endurance
that strength of his arms and back
that unworded smile of his disappointment.

THE DISAPPEARANCE OF JOHN

A young woman is working over her husband.
He's becoming a statue. She hammers away, shouting,
"John, John, I know you can hear me. John?"
But even as she hammers, he's slipping
into stone. He is not escaping, he knows,
the blood is ceasing to flow, replaced
bit by bit by stone.
Already his eyes appear to be fading,
that feverish glow of anxiety gone. "John?
Are you in there?" and the chisel in haste
placed just center of the shoulder blades,
"John?"
Staring at the resultant dust
on her kitchen floor, she stamps her foot,
"John, this has gone too far!"
before she sweeps him up, and stores
what remains in a silver jar.

INTONATION

In the last of the daylight
the harbor opens like a door,
and jet black cormorants
bloom from the boat.
I feel frightened by their flight,
as if things are not what they seem,
something changing inside me,
a dream, words falling in my throat.
Wing and wing we are peeling
toward gulls. The sun is failing
in an acid haze. We move with a host
of fiberglass boats, the deep water bells
like someone calling.

ALL PIECES OF A LEGACY

You receive the memories, the hunger,
and the dreams shiny as the eyes of madmen
before stately antebellum mansions,
even for the poor more than they were,
like lightning bugs stuck to a summer evening.

Patterns like footprints in the grass
of a barefooted run with June bug
on a string, like a child hugged in the arms
of motherhood, tied to a solid, hard-backed green,
the buzzing, broken as first sex in the back of a car.

And you remember the funny talk of poontang
in barber shops before the hunt begins,
the talk of the remorseless chicken thief,
the hungry coon sought after in the night
out beyond the chinaberry tree, the mimosa
and crepe myrtle, out beyond even the dogwood

through the kudzu, hunted and smiling
from the pine tree, smiling at the dogs
pulled with chains from the moon-cut pine;
you remember that trapped and smiling, high-up coon,
you remember the hunger that would not cease, cease.

THE PALACE OF NEW BEGINNINGS

Alison wanted to believe that words made no difference, but words were her weakness. She had agreed to see him.

She stared at the snow. The apartment grew cold. The couch suddenly became ugly, a brown that made no sense, wouldn't ever die out, a brown she watched spreading around her holding the room to the carpet. At first it was like drowning in air, a slipping inside oneself feeling the darkness close as though a zipper were being shut. But then like a wave leveling back into the body of a lake, her emotions retreated. The couch remained a thing of cushions and legs, a matter of ordinary experience. Outside it continued to snow.

Alison Benet was thirty-three. She had one child, David Benet, was now separated from her husband, John David Benet. It was midnight, but even so she decided to bathe and wash her hair. John would be coming tomorrow. She began to undress where she stood. The snow would not stick. Tomorrow would be a mess. Her body tingled from the chill on the room. Yes, she had grown thin. She lifted one breast and examined it, let it fall. Her body seemed a separate thing to her, something that lived, breathed, felt of its own will. It had not always been so. She had been young once. When? How long ago? She stared at the veins, just visible coursing blue tracks, her breast rising with her breathing. John would be coming. For an instant his large face on the pillow. She had been young once. Tomorrow he was coming. No, she did not hate him. All at once she wanted to laugh. Why had she agreed to see him? Because she needed to see him again, she thought, once more, know him, know his hands on her, know for the last time he meant nothing to her.

. . . .

John David rises alone. It's early morning. The clatter of his dressing fills the cabin. Tennis shoes padding to a square kitchen sink. In a mirror the size of his hand he brushes his teeth, splashes water at his face. It's cold, ice cold. He smiles. His large face does not fit the mirror. Two rows of teeth, pieces of grinning cheek, open large nostrils bring him the morning.

Outside he begins to run. One lap of the lake. Three miles. It has taken him two months to build up to it. The right distance, he had decided, enough given, enough taken away. The cottonwoods around the lake loom up stark and pale out of the white morning. He crosses the ruins of a barbed wire fence, descends a small incline, and begins to run again. Soon the heavy snow will come. The lake will freeze over and his routine will be broken. But for now, again he settles into the pace. The muffled steps of his running lift into stillness.

A slow warmth spreads through his arms and legs. His glasses grow opaque in the cold. He knows this path. Barren, half-white trees lift over him dripping with snow. He runs, half-perceived images striking at the edges of his vision, and the outside world of lake, trees, and snow begins to slip away. He would be with her in a few hours. They had been separated almost three months now. Why did he want to see her again? Why had he talked her into it? He imagined her running naked before him in the snow. He wanted her. He couldn't help himself. In his mind he was chasing her, but she was like a bird, pretending she was hurt, leading him away from something, something she did not want him to find. And he followed her, her heavy blond hair over her back, laughing at him now, he wanted her, his breath coming faster, the way she danced, and suddenly he was running and she was afraid. He would take her now. She could not last and he was running flat out, he would have her, flat out into nothingness.

Where the path curved back to his cabin he came to a halt. Immediately he was cold. Overhead a shaftless arrow of ducks going South. Suddenly Alison was a reality again.

. . . .

She placed two blouses on her bed—David had spent the night with his grandparents—and walked to the window wearing jeans and sandals. Already the snow was melting. It remained piled only in shadows. The coffee pot began crackling on the stove. She poured herself a second cup, but did not drink any. Returned to her bedroom and rejected the Mexican print for the white silk. Then, before the mirror, tortoise-shell rose tinted glasses, peacock feather ear-rings, no bra, her blond hair tied in a loose braid, she thought, it's not a matter of deception, but of pleasure. Why did it take me so long to discover that? She returned to her coffee, but it was cold. She poured it out, turned the burner on low, he would be arriving any minute now. She sat down to wait.

. . . .

John David Benet roared to a stop before the florist's shop, raced the engine once and turned it off. For a moment he seemed a night rider, a vision of death and destruction. Off came his mask, his rain suit glistening, and he ran inside to return with a dozen long stemmed roses. Then even the roar of his cycle seemed the expression of something gentle, a dream discovered to be reality, a simple man on a simple journey.

. . . .

At the door to her apartment he suddenly became nervous. A presentiment. She would refuse him. In a rush he saw it all. She would be dressed up, the apartment clean, and David would be gone, staying with her parents again. It was a set up. She would refuse him. He looked down at his clothes. They seemed baggy and ill-formed. Behind the door she would be waiting, beautiful, waiting for him to try something, waiting to refuse him. He felt ridiculous. He wanted to put on his rainsuit again, his helmet, rush through the door and attack her as she stood with her hand still stretched out to him. Suddenly he wanted to leave, sneak down the stairs, and leave. She would refuse him. That thought spinning around and around finally dropped inside him like an anchor. He felt it sinking, felt the line grow taut, and placing his motorcycle gear on the floor, lifting the roses before him, he knocked on the door. On hearing the rustle of her approach, a hot wave rushed at his face.

. . . .

The roses in a blue vase between them, they seemed unable to find the right tact for conversation.

"How's David?" he said, and looked around the room as though expecting to find him hidden somewhere, his gaze finally coming to rest on a tiny racing car wedged under the credenza.

"He's fine," she said, "he wanted to spend the night with my parents." There was a tone of self-defense to her voice which she did not like.

He smiled, grimly.

And then, "You're looking beautiful today," without looking at her, the words like a challenge. And he could not look at her, her nipples clearly visible beneath the silk, noticed the racing car was missing a wheel, wanted to take down her hair, run his hands under her breasts, was grateful for the roses between them.

And she accepted the challenge. She *was* beautiful today. She knew it, knew it as a pleasure that tingled inside her, knew he could not look at her, knew it and reached forward, pushed the roses over to one side, said, "Well, now let me have a look at you."

Alice Fulton

THE CHANGELINGS

Although she wanted trust
worthy men who wore rubbers, sold insurance,
she always found herself with con men
who wanted to take parts of her
body a hand or breast in black and white.
Pin-striped changelings with minnow eyes.
There was one who carried gold toothpicks,
all night ground his teeth, mouth tight
as a baby's curled fist. Then
attracted by the quiet hum
of the pocket calculator in his pants,
she seduced an accountant but
putting an ear to his chest found
his heart, gray and slimy as an oyster.
Tried to love an undertaker who stood to
inherit his father's business, discovered
his skin had no seams, black vinyl
dreams in bondage under his lids.
At last, met a man with hair like a moth's fur
who watched birds and wore a golden crucifix.
It wasn't until she said I love you
that she felt the nubs under his shoulder
blades like antlers budding.
She had to put her coat on
over her nightgown escape
before wings sprouted & shred
the sheets like old wedding gowns
filling up her life with lint.

Richard Wyatt

FARMER RETURNING HOME AT EVENING TIME

A lone bird trails threads of silence
Across the still sky
Hangs
For a moment
Then moves on

The smell of orange blossoms blooming
Along the road
A gentle thief
Steals my thought a moment
Then is gone

Childhood
Youth
Old age
I once thought like footsteps
Leading to god

But now old past my years
Each evening time I
wearily wrench myself from the earth
Half-bent
Like some old iron nail
I start for home
singing

Allah why
Do my days plod like
Oxen towards you
Allah could
The yoke of my suffering
Be too much of a burden

BODHISATTVA GRANDMA

by the picket fence
beneath the jacaranda tree
madder than any
fire engine racing
down dawn streets
your silence

JoAnn Ugolini

ACROSS THIS ROOM

For a minute
forget
the sundays
that were not
what we expected
the gray sleep
the slow sunday
faces the

time you said
life is simple
and I thought
of a trail of
smoke on a
slow train
the train that's
vanished

since you said it
now your back
is marginal
and hard to trace
your fingers unfamiliar
tucking in
the edges
of your shirt

your shirt is blue
it's all I see
of you the sundays
are behind us.

I'VE HAD ENOUGH OF THESE FOUR WALLS

"I've had enough of these four walls," she said. And she grabbed her
coat, threw it over her shoulder, and tossed back her head. That was
the last scene of the last movie I ever saw. After that there was no
need to see any more movies.

In the laundromat there is an old woman who sits around making wisecracks at little kids. At first the kids think she's joking so they stick around until she tells them to fuck off.

I moved to an apartment building with a laundry room so there's no need to go to the laundromat anymore but sometimes I go anyway just to hear what insults the old woman will hurl next, and to watch the kids' faces changing.

My apartment building is pink with red geraniums in two pots outside the front gate. Every day when I walk past them I imagine I'm the woman in the movie and bit by bit I pick another flower off a stem, flick it into the gutter, and toss back my head.

John Yurechko

NIGHT TERM

night term yeah thats a pisser
those fuckin cock suckers wont let a man work decent time and
sleep when youre supposed too
jesus fuck what the hell do dey expect
shit says tony bengeeny the italian
here comes that polish cock suck
mike frakor the foreman
kiss his ass the big prick
walks around like hes got a shovel up his bun
so the big shit walks right up to me
scratches his crotch
spits
and pushes his smelly polish face up against mine
are you a good fuckin worker or a bad fuckin worker
cause i aint got no time for some shitass kid whos gonna
fuckoff on my time he says
we give youse guys a good eight hours pay and expect a good eight
                                                    hours work
'fuckayou mike the italian says
the skinny wild eyes buck toothed rumanian shrimp
steps out of the gang and pulls down his zipper
whips out his cock says
suck on dis mike deres a good eight hours work dere and plenty to
                                                    spare
for the old lady
yeah
grotesque laughter ruffles the graphite and the whole fuckin crew
pounds their hardhats on the cement for the show
frakor calls out 60471 third helper
and wallace says i dont wanna go third helper let bengeeny go
that italian cunt scratcher
get the fuck up there before i send you home you hunky
                                          motherfucker
jesus youse guys i kiss your ass and you turn around and piss in my
                                                    face
mikes a dicky licker someone adds
the rumanian still has his cock out and proceeds to piss in the corner
a rat scurries across the floor and bengeeny grabs a brick and beans
                                                    the fucker

it isnt dead but out cold
frakors on the phone so the whole fuckin crew 20 men or so
go over to the furnace (theres nine of them big fuckers filled with
                                            molten steel
as big as a house)
the rumanian opens one of the seven furnace doors yeah
and fuckin tony the italian has got the rat by the tail yeah and its
                                            comin to
so he starts to swing it over his head yeah shit and we're all laughing
our fuckin balls off while the rumanian turns the furnace up to
                                            2800⁰
yeah do it you fuckin italian do it bengeeny
so he whips the fuckin rat squealing into the furnace
right on top of 750 tons of molten steel
and you shoulda seen it yeah why that little fucker ran 15 feet
                                            before
he just fartified (thats what we call it when he just turns into
                                            gas and poof
yeah ya shoulda seen it just kinda shriveled up like a prune and
                                            poof
most of the time they get about 5 or 10 feet but that pisser was a
                                            champ
frakor comes back with his safety glasses hanging from his left
                                            ear over his mouth
30146 (shit thats me with that fuckin open hearth number)
go pit side
shit Mike

Laura Moriarty

EVENT POEMS

I. *Summer People*

We would all walk around the center
leaving large footprints in the sand.

The inexperienced would cast the nets
and the children would serve the pig.

We would go naked to embarrass ourselves and
everyone would try to keep his face straight.

The quahog shells would be saved, naturally
we would gather periwinkles.

There would be a lot of wine and
a few of us would get lost in the dunes.

The children would rise early and
find us huddled against a white hillock.

They would always look the same and
we would call them names like "Tommy" and "Dierdre".

We would do this several times
before returning for the winter.

II. *Luncheon*

We would lunch at the
renovated smalltown.

I have always, you would say,
Yes, it is nice.

An acquaintance, Persian, of yours, good
English for only, yes indeed, would appear or

would be spoken of. The music,
yes, the digestion and atmosphere.

Oh yes, I've, Persian would always agree,
one noticed eventually.

Secret cheesecake. They actually won't?
No, not a word, an old family.

Next, why not, of course,
Thursday afternoon.

I have always, you would say,
Yes it is nice.

III. *Dinner Party*

We would cook flesh and
vegetables in white wine and cream.

The glasses would be full
and the soup tureen with its silver ladle.

Our black suits and gowns would
look well in the white room.

We would speak French or
in French sounds and nod and smile.

Our laughter would be clear light
rings of silver and china.

During brandy we would speak of
our children, making up ages and names.

We would drive away in swift,
enormous cars, silently.

We would do this every month.

COLDSNAP

If walking I look down
and imagine my feet bleeding,
cut by bladed leaves
lying beneath the eucalyptus,
it is only the atmosphere
of this frozen tree
which leads me to such
unnecessary connections.

For the frost
from which this tree
recoiling
was surprised into death
is really unlike
anything
that ever passed between us.

WIDOW'S LAMENT

As the snow fills this canyon
and river's bed and the white lasts,
so our room was white within its blue.
This white I creased as
more frost darkened the windowpane.
But I never made you welcome
in these linens.   The thick odor of your
starched underclothes.   Your deals
and broadcloth wink of ownership.
The caloused whiskey cradle
of your cracked palm peeled
as you ran your hand over me.

The newsprint faded
as the steaming cups
and lacquered tray of haze
began to blue and obscure,
and the hard oiled panels blued
also until the house,
resined in its own grain,
closed up your remaining husk.
And I, having waited so long for this,
was not even left alive.

———————

In the morning I wash my hair,
shivering into the shower still asleep.
Read or go back to sleep or
masturbate for awhile until it is
partly dried. Stroking, hot air
and bristles separating each hair.
My head bent, my face hidden by warm
plaits of just damp hair drying
from a dark wet into a light brown.
Soft in the morning, smooth after brushing,
a dull shine and soft clean wave.

But if you are there in the morning
and I slip away and come back
to warm beside you, wet hairs sticking
to my face and neck, my hair dries
in wrinkled bunches, frizzing at the ends
and looks all day bushy, wild.

Phyllis Koestenbaum

I MEET JOE SCHWARTZ AT THE SYMPHONY

my son introduces him
his name is Joe
he has a mustache
and his skin is new
I think his hand is thin as chicken bones
how young I feel
squealing my robin's breaths
how are you Joe
won't you come to lunch

> I am straw
>
> I am my mahogany piano
> slick with forty years of Johnson's wax
>
> I am branches growing wild
> from streams flowing mud
> like menopausal periods
>
> I am the shock of morning water
> so I run in fast
> to get it over with
>
> I am the wetness of the midnight grass
> in Prospect Park
> making love on newspapers
>
> I am a peach
> if you touch my afternoon skin
> it bruises
> and the juices pour out sucking tart

I cannot be someone's mother
feeling like this

> the yellow carpet in the concert hall
> is turning black
> with footsteps staining side by side
>
> the stage is collapsing

sixty black suit strings
are playing Cage
where the score clearly calls for Bach

and now no notes at all
just din and howl and pound

Lyn Lifshin

THE MAN IN
THE BOILER ROOM

is drilling holes
behind the bed
he's fixing the
furnace he's making
the holes so he
can see he's not
taking chances
working slowly
making a lot of
them he sees her
blue sheets with
yellow flowers
when she leaves
for a class he
pushes a window
comes in and smells
her clothes he
knows what pills
are in the drawer
he makes the holes
bigger She dreams
of a man under the
bed just like we
all do He's
getting ready She
imagines hands
but not on her
mouth hard pulling
all the phones
the light
wires dead

Bruce Horovitz

GOING THROUGH LINCOLN'S POCKETS

> A mystery box containing the things Abraham Lincoln carried in his pockets when he was assassinated was opened yesterday on Lincoln's birthday in celebration of the bicentennial year.
>
> *San Francisco Chronicle* Feb. 13, 1976

The string had no life at all,
and the brown wrapping looked to have been sealed
by a woman. The corners were tucked in,
and each side was even. Years
of folds showed age, like an elected man.

The box was opened upside-down, and the things
that once filled his pockets, fell,
after 102 years of being inside. A pair
of eyeglasses had already been broken; one
temple-piece held taut by a string. A white
handkerchief (still white) fell in a queer way,
and where embroidery should have initialed,
it spelled out Abraham Lincoln, just as
a familiar man would have spoken his name.

A president had to look like he carried
a watch, but the watch-fob was naked,
and he never considered it being
in his pocket. Something was scratched
or engraved on his penknife, and he never
considered it, either.

Newspaper clippings folded into airy print;
a headline read: DISAFFECTION AMONG SOUTHERN SOLDIERS.
The words tore through his head
like a well-aimed bullet;
the remains were gathered and boxed.

Dorothy Bryant

SOMETHING COMING

George, of course, just yelled when he found out. Forgot his arthritis and swung in here, right past the nurses, stood over me and started yelling. "I'll be broke, in debt, in disgrace. You did it, and I'll pay the price."

As usual he couldn't see anything but his own problem. I told him, life is full of surprises, most of them unpleasant. When I married you, fourteen years older than I, everyone said I'd be left a lonely old widow some day. But the things you worry about never happen. Other things do.

"Revenge! You never forgave me for Emmy, even though that was fifteen years ago and I never saw her again!"

"Revenge? That's silly. How did I know I was going to die of cancer at forty-nine. If I hadn't gotten sick, no one would have known, least of all you, George. You'd have died happy in a few more years, content in knowing I'd give you a fine funeral. As for Emmy, I've probably missed her more than you have. She was my friend, after all."

He started yelling again. The nurse came in and said he'd have to quiet down; he was disturbing the other patients. Not a word about disturbing me. And she never looks me in the eye. None of them do. That's how I knew before the doctor told me. The minute I woke up from the surgery, the way the nurse in the recovery room looked at me, I knew I was a dead woman.

"I don't know you," he said, a little quieter. "Married thirty-one years, and I never knew you."

That's not news to me. I used to say it to myself at least once every day of those thirty-one years. What made me sad was that you thought you did. Everybody thought they did, as if there wasn't much to know. I started thinking so too. Until these last few years when I knew there was more than . . . oh, well, no hard feelings. Probably two people couldn't live together for thirty-one years if they really knew each other.

"How could you do this to me!"

George, I didn't do anything to you. When you think about it, you'll realize your perspective's all wrong. To me, it seems that you got all the benefits, none of the trouble. I shared all the money with you and none of the disgrace. Nobody's going to make you pay it back. They'll feel sorry for you. Because of your reduced standard of living. So you got a free ride. Early retirement and travel, and the Tahoe cabin (yes, that's mortgaged too, no equity at all) and the season tickets and the Mercedes (you're getting too old to drive anyway). You know I never cared about things like that. It was you who always talked about going to Tahiti. So I gave you the whole South Pacific with Japan thrown in for good measure. I never really enjoyed it. I'd have been just as happy staying right at home here in Berkeley, if it hadn't changed so no decent person could be happy here.

So then he kind of sagged and winced as he bent his knees and sat down. He looked down at the floor and started sighing the way he did the time our daughter announced she was having a baby. A black baby. As usual he gave up, sitting and sighing, and I had to make all the abortion arrangements. I knew Susie just wanted to scare us again and didn't have any intention of getting saddled with a baby, black or white. But sigh as he will, there's nothing I can do about it this time. Dying is full time, and I can't take time out to worry about him. He's already had fourteen more years than I'm going to have, and maybe a lot more. Thin years, granted. But alive. If I were him, I wouldn't waste a minute of them yelling at me.

Finally he got up and said he couldn't forgive me for what I'd done. "But I won't leave you to die alone."

Alone, I told him, is the only way anyone dies. I was just mentioning something I'd learned, now that I'm an authority, just giving information. But he was offended and looked as if he might start yelling again, so I closed my eyes.

After he left, Susie called. I guess he must have let her know. I can't think how. Most of the time the phone is disconnected, like the plumbing and the people, at that communal slum, that holy farm, where this year she is growing wormy potatoes and meditating. I haven't seen her since our thirtieth wedding anniversary party at the Claremont Hotel, for which occasion she showed up to greet our 400 guests with her head shaved. Now there's revenge, if George wants revenge. She has been relentlessly revenging herself on us since she was thirteen. Why? I stopped asking why about her or anything else, a long time ago. But now I have at least the answer to the question, how do you get a friendly phone call from your twenty-eight year old daughter? Drop dead. I was afraid she would want to help me die in the benefits of her new religion, but, as it turned out, she didn't mention that at all.

"How'd you do it, Mom?"

Do what? Oh, the money. I just borrowed. You know all the old houses people left when Berkeley changed, and they moved out and rented them to groups of people like . . . like you and your friends. I started managing them, as a favor to old clients and friends who don't exactly relish dealing with a certain type of tenant. They were all free and clear. I mortgaged them.

"You forged the owner's signature?"

And then there were some who gave me money to invest for them. Without a note, that's right. People who've known me, dealt with me since you were in diapers. Who knows more about property and investments in Berkeley?

"And nobody ever suspected . . ."

What was there to suspect? I was keeping up the payments on all the loans, giving twelve percent on the money people gave me to invest. Everybody was happy. If I hadn't gotten sick . . .

"As simple as that?" A new tone in Susie's voice. Not only lack of hate. Respect? As if for the first time since I helped her with her multiplication tables, I had given her some useful information. "Is it that easy?"

For me. It wouldn't work for you, or for your friends. You have to be a stable person, with a business built over a lifetime. A respectable person, not allergic to putting in hours and hours, every day for years. With courtesy, good manners, proper dress. Oh, you don't know what I'm talking about. No decent person in this town would question a signature on a contract I brought in. But it takes the best years of your life to build trust like that. And I gave them. So my word was enough. For ten years I was chairman of the Ethics Committee of the Real Estate Board.

She started laughing, and that didn't bother me because from my new point of view I see the irony of many things, my life among them. I would have laughed with her for the first time in fifteen years if I didn't know that any move would wake up the pain sleeping under the last hypo the nurse gave me. Then she sounded as if her laugh would end, and she was going to say something I've waited years to hear, but I suddenly felt afraid of hearing because it would wake up even deeper pain. So I asked her if she planned to come to my funeral naked and, in the middle of *that* laugh, I hung up.

I closed my eyes again and thought about the minister's visit and the way he just ran on nervously until I asked him if George hadn't told him what I'd done. "Yes," he said, "but my concern is with your immortal soul, not with money." I'd warned them they were hiring a radical when they got this new young man. They'll see. Anyone who'll dismiss money that way will soon have guitars and incense, like all the others.

We prayed for a while, and then he stood up, took my hand, and said, "I'm sure people will remember you only for all the good you did." I'm sure he meant to comfort me, but he made me feel just the opposite. Maybe with his attitude and George's fear of disgrace, and Brenda's fear for the business, the whole thing will just be hushed up. I never thought about that before. I never thought of whether I would or wouldn't want people to know, after I'm gone. For so long, it was my special secret. The excitement of knowing, even the bit of fear of what would happen if they found out. And the fun of dropping hints nobody ever picked up because I was above suspicion. That was more than the money. I never cared about the money. But after I'm dead, they should know. Give credit where credit is due.

Brenda came again this afternoon, faithful as ever. Twenty years we worked together, talked together, drank together. Many times she told me, when her husband died she would have killed herself if it hadn't been for me. She was the one who put me up for the Ethics Committee. I told her, listen, Brenda, we always wore the same size, and I've got that new two hundred dollar pant suit. You take it before I'm gone and George's sisters descend on the place.

She shook her head, and took out a piece of paper and a pen. "So far we've traced seventeen of them. Here are the names. Now, which ones don't we know?"

I closed my eyes again.

Brenda started to cry, and I really did feel sorry. She's not young anymore, and this was a big shock to her. She smelled of Scotch every time she came, even in the morning. I told her yesterday if she keeps this up, she won't last much longer after I go. Who'll nag her about her drinking after I'm gone? I like Brenda. But she's not very bright. I thought she'd never catch on. Every day she'd call the hospital, asking, "Shall I call Gleason? Their loan payment hasn't come in and it's already the tenth." And I'd tell her, don't worry, they're not a bunch of damned hippies, don't bother them, they'll pay. I knew it would all come out now, and maybe I should have broken the news to Brenda myself. But I'd just heard my own bad news, and I was too busy thinking about that.

"Why don't you tell me about the others?"

I felt too tired to open my eyes. Why hurry? She'll find out anyway, one at a time, when the rest of them call. Maybe some of them won't. Maybe old friends, for George's sake. And what's a few thousand to them anyway? Some of them, for old time's sake, might just pay off the loan and keep quiet. Some will just write off what they gave me, ashamed to mention they gave me money without a note. Oh. I wonder if someone might just step forward and pretend they gave me money, trying to collect. Now, I call that dishonest. At least I was paying back.

"You never thought about being sent to prison?"

I just kept my eyes closed and shook my head. And, though I meant to say nothing, I found myself telling Brenda about that little mouse who worked in George's office. She did everything but brush his teeth for him, and he called her Miss Indispensible, and she'd blush and squint behind her glasses and scurry back behind her desk. She took over a hundred a month out of petty cash for more than ten years before he caught her. Cornered, she brazened it out, saying she hadn't had a raise for fifteen years, and she just took what was coming to her. She didn't go to prison. George just fired her and then complained he could never find anyone as efficient.

I opened my eyes to see if Brenda got the point. But she was just looking at me like I was crazy as well as dead. So I didn't tell her what I was feeling, that no matter how much more I made than Miss Indispensible, I always felt the same way: I had something coming to me, and when was it finally going to come?

No, they wouldn't send me to prison, I told Brenda. Even if I was going to live long enough. Why, at my trial, there'd be dozens of character witnesses. All the good I've done for this city all my life, the committees I worked on, the candidates I helped elect, at least back before the radicals took over everything. And the contributions. They'd be amazed how much of that money I gave to charity. What was I going to do with it? We couldn't travel much anymore with George's arthritis and my having to keep my eye on all the payments. And what can you do with money except buy dinners you can't eat anymore, shows that give you a headache, clothes you'll never wear out.

Brenda had started crying again, when the door opened and the Gleasons marched in. I knew they'd show up. Most of the others would be ashamed to bother a dying woman, but not them. Frank and Abigail Gleason. Over thirty-eight thousand. Not that they can't afford it. Didn't I sell them four apartment houses in Alameda, where there aren't any tenants' unions or trouble about keeping out blacks and long-hairs? And managed it all myself, for old time's sake, without charging them a dime. So I did mortgage one of them . . . two? Anyway the others are still free and clear and bringing in good rents. They won't live forever. And they won't find anyone to manage their apartments as well as I did.

Frank looked stern and dignified, aloof, the way he has ever since he went deaf. Abigail was twitching around the mouth, but she was always too much of a lady to make direct complaints so for a while they both just sat there, looking across the room about a foot above my body stretched out there between them. Old, old Berkeley, the two of them, as opposed to just old Berkeley, lying here dying of cancer at forty-nine. I used to wonder if my hair would turn as white-white as Abigail's some day, and then would I blue it and lean on my ornamented cane and talk of the days at Anna Head School before it dissolved with all the other decent values and places. Of course, Abigail always acted as if the school had gone pretty far downhill before I went there, but, still, she gave me a look that said an old Anna Head girl couldn't have done what I did.

Then she finally got out one word. "Why?"

And all of a sudden, even with my eyes still open, all I could see was that black boy we caught carrying out our color television. We didn't know what to do. He only looked about thirteen, and we didn't want to call the police. George held on to him, shaking him and yelling. But I tried to look at him in a kindly way. I asked him, why?

That dark, furious look he turned on me. I never forgot it. Then he said, "I wanted it." And I could see he was lying, or maybe he didn't know why. So then we called the police, but he didn't go to prison either, was only put on probation, because there's no room to put him and all the others like him and Miss Indispensible, all the ones who know there's something they've got coming, but it never comes, and besides, they really don't know what it is.

So I just looked at Abigail and said the same thing.

I wanted it.

Then I stared her down till she got up and marched out. That's the only way to talk to people who ask, why? Everyone who asks, why, is lying too, but won't admit it. I don't have to ask or wonder why, because pretty soon I'll know everything. That's what the minister said. I hope he's wrong.

Roswell Spafford

QUESTIONS, ANSWERS

I.

We share stories, afterward.
Your life sounds like fiction, I am so removed from it.
I see only the moist imprints from your body,
your silver trail across my belly,
the tiny thumbprint bruise.

Later, I stare across the low table
at the bones in your wife's face,
try to talk a little with her.
Her wrists circle in the air,
her voice flutters,
but it is clear she is not a light woman.

I imagine the two of you as lovers,
hand in hand on the set of a foreign film
from another time.

I sit here, now, in your kitchen.
the fiction has become the open landscape of your shared rooms.
I am wondering why I am here,
cannot remember your body,
or see the lines that connect our three lives.

II.

Those long nights, when we lay side by side
listening to jazz records,
listening for the sound of the key,
listening with our bodies to the tension :
> It hums like the thick string on the curved wood bass.
> It moans like the saxophone,
> like the woman in the night.

What does it mean, the quartets and sequences of bodies ?
What are the spontaneous frequencies
that penetrate, play us, leave ?

III.

The jazz that sounds like movie themes
plays while the woman drives the country road.
She is driving to meet a man

or away from one, thinking:
    What was that; for how long;
    What am I doing?
and the trees flow by unseen,
        and the days,
until someone's eyes at an intersection
remind her she is driving,
remind her she is going someplace.

MUDSLIDE, TANGLEBLUE RIDGE

This is the way things slide away from us,
recollections, certainties

In March
when the old roots rot
or grow too shallow to bind the snow soaked clay
to the hill
and it begins to slide
spills over granite, manzanita, pine

There is no eluding the loss,
the cutting loose.

Now, under the mud-sleek scar,
the old-timers say: pan for gold
wait for it to sift through

What I recover flickers in the rust palm
of my washing pan
priceless, unsure

Bart Alberti

LOCATED

I.

Life is an old mortgage that is always running
A corpse filed in the county clerk's office
A deed that the coroner examines
The poet wrote
"Brown hair is sweet
Brown hair over the mouth
Lilac and brown hair"
in the evening, the evening, my dear
the evening with the surveyors' maps
that evening with the suicide kit

II.

I walked, my colleague wrote,
"through triste and distal avenues"
past Harve de Grace, Winchester
past York and past Lancaster
past the poet turning on the winding stair
the poet with the bowl of white carnations
in Connecticut

III.

there is a stricture in the stream of poetry
we perform a ligation
distal to the point
mobilizing the affected structures
with probes
mastering the healing art of words
keen
their variation, passion, their subtlety

IV.

The Grande Dame impressive as a Great Dane
surrounded by her jewelled sewing boxes
muff, moustier patterned ware
(her solicitor moving a decree *nisi*)
shoots it up in an upper E. side apt.
is found dead in a jail cell in Chico, Ca.
her husband suing the sheriff in negligence

V.

conversant with secrets
disposed to grant
obliging to the Querent
lilies and roses in the garden
show the cultivation of desire
THE MAGICIAN
the poet, this.

Richard Strong

WALPI, ARIZONA

Peaches, corn, beans and melons.
In 1890 the people wanted wagons and stoves.
They were truly gentle—concerned because
the Navajo were always stealing their horses.

Now they have new ford pickups
and eat peaches from a can—
throw the can tinkling down
the cracks at mesa's edge.

———————

Out in a hot valley town
in some bare bulb kitchen
a working stiff
involved in some nameless
quarrel . . .
pauses in the midst
of everyday beer can snapping anxiety—
shouts at his wife—
trembling with rage
hopeless, weedy and red faced . . .

Later in restrained, oak paneled
judges' chambers
down at the old County Court House
the principals go over the drama
in subdued accents—
flies hover in a pattern
in the air.

Working man cannot understand
why he must go to jail
because he wants to live so much,
so much that it hurts sometimes—
mostly at night
and in the summer time
on hot nights
he feels crazy with it.

DESERT RIVER

Slow brown river winding treeless
across a desert
to dry out on an alkali flat

Olive colored water
past hot gravels,
Stains the noses
of horses dark
after a dusty trip.
Afterwards the clay
dries on fetlocks.

We all go back to the river
and the river
goes back to the sky.

TIRED HORSES

Knowing what's to be done
and knowing the horses are tired
and the bay mare needs shoes,
(my children need shoes).
The year is getting late and—
Great God! the wine is good.

All that is accomplished is living
after all—getting the hay put up
and the cattle moved off the summer range
in the fall of the year.

UTAH MINERS

"Park City Consolidated Mines Company
needs a limited number of miners and muckers
on or before . . . subject to . . . nothing herein
to be construed as a guarantee of continuous employment."

Time was, when your bull gang WAS SHORT
you hired the first workin' stiff that came along.
It was possible to hear an occasional
healthy : "you're fired"—"You can't fire me, I quit."

You take a mill crew like up at Consolidated:
1 sweeper roaster, 3 pin pointers, 4 trippermen,
5 lug pullers, 3 treater knockers, 3 pug mill operators,
7 slag switchmen, 1 draper silica larryman, 6 slurrygun operators,
3 tong men, 1 skull breaker, and 9 cottrel rectorfiremen.

"Workers of the world arise!"
("I can't, my back is broken"),
. . . A ten percent permanent partial disability of
twenty weeks compensation . . . at $25.00 per week—
            "I accept."
Settlement of 30% for 18 weeks at $33.00 is the disability of a
thumb.
(In Ely, Nevada copper mine, a man cut off a finger
to get a down payment on a new Pontiac).

The cost of timbering is too high nowadays,
better anyway to gob a stope,
you get a better mine out of it
in the end.

But even so, wages aren't high . . .
less than a common laborer's:
two fifty an hour and no over time—
because of the cost of a new shaft—so they say.

They don't like it down at the hall.
Welsh and Scots miners' faces—serious and sober.
Alex Gibson, Pat Smyth, Thomas Grose, William Bates,
John Brierly, and Brother Matt Leahy.

Hilda Johnston

HULK

The boys lie among dirty clothes, sunlight, plastic men,
                                                    stolen tirecaps
reading comic after comic (one hundred eighty-nine this April)
about incredible, monstrous, rampaging Hulk
whose brute skin is green
                                        as the new leaves
whose brute hair is green
                                        as the sourgrass which cracks sidewalks
as Hulk breaks through iron walls,
                                        stops propellers,
halts bullets and missiles of puny humans
like Doctor Bruce Banner, atomic scientist,
                                        Hulk's other self,
smart but afraid. "Hulk knows Hulk's not smart,"
but as the boys say, "he strong nothing don't hurt him"
"Hulk's specialty is smashing." Hulk can squash a truck
easy as a drunk pulls the phone off the wall,
as water cuts stone
                        as spring blasted Van Gogh
through the walls of Saint Rémy. "But he not mean—"
Hulk cried when a girl called him dumb. And when The Stranger
said Earth was too great a danger
                                        to the sprawling universe
and must be destroyed,
                        "Hulk took up for Earth."

William Zander

SILENCE
For Frank Pein, and myself

Even the greatest silent movies needed
something more than Keaton, Lloyd, or Chaplin—
someone, usually not at all a genius,
thumping the keys, slower or faster
as the scene demanded. Even now,
when one might wish for silence
(fed up with modern noise), imagine
seeing those films in perfect silence—
bound and gagged, not even having the solace
of your own laughter in the dark
and soundproof room. Silence!
and another world unfolds, as chilling
as a city siren, hovering, ominous
as an eagle with a snake,
the unshared images of dreams,
the allegory of the cave
but without meaning— watching, watching
with bitter longing and elation,
knowing at last that Truth is distance—
as if this light were all in all,
this black and white, these glowing
pratfalls, wringings of hands,
the chase— they see the efforts
of fools at best, of empty forms at worst,
and only you can see it, only you
are like the universe, with nothing else
to turn to. And now it floats there, hours, days,
like sunlight on the arctic snow.
Listen! Not even a birdsong.
This could be Nothing, but you feel it.
This is reality. This is you.

NO ONE

No one dreams what his death consists of:
always he dreams of falling, or losing
his self-possession, as if appearing

in underwear in public
would kill him. No one is unwatched;
everyone sees his task, a series
of rooms to find his way in.
No one dreams he has his own
spaces, where nightmares come from.
Breathing again, he thinks
he has plumbed the depths, as if
his childhood with its bloody noses
had its place there. Everyone dreams
his story, different from all the others;
different from what the others see,
himself the other. Everyone dreams
he is the watcher. No one
dreams what his death consists of.

Rod Tulloss

PALO ALTO
Variation on a poem by Ken Lewes

Brown and darker brown and three miles off,
the hills rise up
beyond this tidal meadow's whispering grass.
The grass talks
in its sleep, shifts
an arm or leg.
A constant wind is showing us : Look !
This is the earth's strength
rippling and patient, turning
in its sleep.
Now swallows and their paths lacing air —
Now
you feel the flatness of this green place.
Now you remember an old dream :

Stark winter trees,
birds suddenly shooting
across patches of pale sky
a tiny fear turning out of sleep.
Something you wanted to keep fails
like a worn-out heart.
Dry fingers are folded.
A coffin lid is closed.
You're saying, "Maybe *this*
is the last one who'll die. *That*
would be simple." —
like the cereus blooming that one summer night
like its singular grace, its
unthinkable wax petals,
its fragrance
all raised from apparent death.
If only death and old memory
could be caught like a wasp
under an up-turned cup.

No.   No.
We ride a long wave.
The grass isn't listening.

And the salt marsh breathes in sleep
under birds
and the wind blowing

DECEMBER FISHING
for Mark and David

Deep in the dark cold,
carp believe the world is flat,
weighing down on them; the
carp believe silence sits in a cold, stiff chair,
gripping the arms,
panting and goggle-eyed;
and carp believe a bit of worm will cure them
of their scales and gills and foul-smelling skin
so they'll fly up like birds,
like manna with
a return ticket.

A DREAM OF OWLS

Stiff-legged as a feathery hat rack,
it dumbly watches me come round the low black branches

of a pine,
its eyes beaming a gray idiot's light.
It is so large I, at first, take it for a child.
But it is an immense owl—
Like a piece of slow-witted Victorian furniture.
Its wings are terribly small—newly hatched, covered
with millions of tiny bales of cotton.
I awake with all my education packed . . .
and no ticket.

THE FARMER'S CHILDREN

The porcupines are drawn
to human salt licks
on the dying farms.
America has found a sport better than football.

Plymouth Rock has hatched—hair of wild animals
    matted with blood and clay and
tiny birds with the faces of old indian-fighters.
They fly into our mouths when we sleep.
The hair falls into our meats and in the printer's ink.
It causes beautiful new words to appear in the newspapers;
they lie voluptuously in the mouth—
"death orchard"—
it is like velvet on our bodies.
Butchers and college professors
stroke themselves with these words.
They think a knife or a bullet enters a man
like Huck Finn's toes going into mud.
In the Department of Agriculture there is a box of small
                                        gray stones.
Tomorrow they will offer them to us in exchange for our
                                        children.
We have had two presidents in a row
who placed their children in an old volksbus
on a hill
and released the emergency brake.

NEAR OVID MICHIGAN

The roof lines of barns have cut the farmers' throats.
Ovid is the man from the Department of Agriculture who
                comes to take the farm.
In College he wrote sonnets, wanted to help people.
At night, when ghosts of farm dogs wake him,
he sharpens his pencils to a heap of shavings.

NIGHT·DRIVING

In every low place, there is fog—
ancestor of the continents—
sucking at the headlights.
On higher ground, rotting silos, gasping like asthmatics
    in the heavy air.
These are the quaint stone farms dropped on the Indians.

FIRST MONTHS

He fails to shave,
and I curse his ugliness because my belly is growing again.
In my sleep that tastes of bile,
I dream of coarse men unloading sides of beef into a wet street.
All movies stutter backward,
and butterflies crawl into cocoons and die.

I want to hibernate, small and afraid, in the middle of a loaf of bread
and grow warm, soft fur all over my body
and be completely alone in a tiny house like dust, not even dreaming;
but this small fishthing turns a heavy gauge screw in my womb.

I cry for my heart, battered by lower guts, a small animal pummeled
        by brutal children,
and for the warm, wet shame that runs down my thighs as my husk
tries
        to empty its emptiness again.

POEM IN IMITATION OF
MANY "YOUNG POETS OF AMERICA"

I

We are very small.
We are at the bottoms of two flower pots.
We are writing identical poems
addressed to each other.
Night is a neolithic super-penguin
defending New York from the steam engine.

II

The tiny mice of electricity
are carrying your name
grain by grain   .
into their hollow nests in light bulbs.
The whole house is filling up with you.
We will eat you
drink you
flush you
read by you
sleep on you and under you
open and close you . . .
Night is a lame crow humping the baby Jesus.

PRO GERTRUDE STEIN

unusual foetus
Columbus Ohio
unusual foetus
Columbus Ohio

Sara Sarley
running barley
barley barely
hardly barley

And all of his wife's family
especially Emily
and if not Emily then hurriedly
and if not hurriedly then not so furry or far.

POEMS THAT FLOAT AWAY

This poem is a feather.
Give it to an editor, and
the slightest draft will take it out a window.
I cannot make it heavier.
I've put in all the rusty scrap I could find—
old cars, cans, clothes dummies, radiators, razor blades,
                                            steam boilers.
Just get a good grip on it!
I'd hate for it to float away with all the rest—twisting,
keeping to the air or rocky streambeds,
shaking us off the trail.
Good God!
It might go bad, buy
a gun and
hold up banks
                and deadlines.
Oh, Lord, how it would hurt
to see my own poem swaggering out of low bars—
eyes full of cruelty!
I wish we didn't have to speak in front of him like this . . .

EVERYTHING YOU NEED TO KNOW

Taking the clay out from under her nails
she says that she's been happy all afternoon, but
always cries
in the morning.
He makes tea.
They don't drink it.
She says he
worries too much, not
enough joy when
they make love.
She says, "Remember everything I say,
but
don't think about it."
He thinks of a knot of hands
full of kindness,
but all pointing in different directions.
She says the intensity
of his love
is desperation, is
a drag.
He can imagine this, but
that knot of gentle hands
is his mind. He thinks
it's hard to change.
She says, "Curl up," and curls
around his back.
They sleep. He's wrong
about a lot
of things.

Betty Coon

SELF-PORTRAIT AT FIFTEEN

The girl stands
beyond the shadow of the orange tree
in a new bathing suit.
Her legs are pressed tightly together;
one hand creeps shyly over her thigh.
Bougainvillea bleeds down a white wall behind.

She wants to walk out of the picture,
but nothing moves.
The sun stays at the same angle;
her small breasts refuse to grow;
her toes curl into the dirt.

NIGHTMARE

All night I've been driving around
a carload of crazies.
An old woman in the backseat
clutches her belly
and yells for a hospital.
She's expecting, has been
for thirty years.
The black woman next to her wants the airport.
She's going to London, Paris, or Ankara.
It doesn't matter where.
In the front seat a teenage girl with acne
sobs into the dash.
"Where are the baby clothes,"
the old woman moans,
"I forgot the baby clothes."
The black woman drums the seat.
"Gonna get myself a ticket a ticket a ticket."
I watch the headlights, the white line.
If I had any guts
I'd run us all into a ditch,
but I could never make it out of this desert
barefoot and alone.

GOING HOME

For Celeste

I drove all night
through truckstops and small towns,
sick from too much love or too little.
Every fifty miles the radio faded into static
and I turned the dial.
From Baja California
a Mexican announcer touted
a remedy for hemorrhoids
at only *tres dollares veinte cinco;*
an announcer in Boise, Idaho
recited the price of sugar beets;
the young in Visalia were advised not to marry.
And always another song about love —
love gone wrong
love without regrets
love that kills
love that restores.
Miles of grapevines in Delano,
then at dawn the road found cottonfields
oil pumps
and the heat rising with the sun
as I turned East toward the desert.
With scarves hanging from their hats
to protect necks from sun
braseros heading into the fields.
Farther east, scrub oak was dry, tough,
and scattered over the brown hills.
Bony Herefords stood around a saltblock.
I drove on
over animals flattened past recognition
on the pavement ˏ
until the land was white in the heat,
mountain after mountain
untouched by green.
For hours I sweated it out
until I found the river,
your adobe house,
my room, cool as the melon you brought me,
even in that heat.

Margaret Teague

R.E.A.

we are driving
through farm country
heavy car
sliding around the hills
far into dark
now and then
we see houses and barns
in their single-pole tents
of harsh light
the black air
sags to the ground between them
My mother says
Think what it was like
out here
before the electricity came
you were really far
from anything
and it was so quiet
when the sun went down.

Nina Rogozen

She said the rain would not fall here,
on this street where the gutters are not wide
and the corner can be two seas crossing.
It will not rain here for I am drunk and without
boots, and my eyelashes have turned to steel, in the open
mouth of night. It will not rain here, the cloud above this
house has dried to a coarse stone, it will not rain !
The barren schoolyard has six shadows, one for the morning and the rest
for the death of five angels, children who were not ready to die,
but could not live in the swallow's mouth. It will not rain here,
there are no hats on the angels, and their mothers' mouths are pressed
to the glass of their windows, waiting for the clouds to break.

In the morning I wake, move slowly towards the window.
As I open the curtains, 5 small doves inch out of a thin crack,
having grown where the rain collected.

Peter Najarian

STORYTIME

One night deep in the old black hole I looked for a little story to take me away, but there was only the usual great stuff, Aeschylus, Tolstoi, and so forth. Hundreds of geniuses were all over the house and I went through the history of misery and redemption like one of the ants in the back yard climbs up the wall, through the floor, up my leg and into my pubic hair looking for something, food, love, God, an orgasm, another ant . . . who knows what? So too did I search, until hero after hero was thrown to the floor defeated by my loneliness. Unfinished and rejected they sprawled at my feet, Modern Library Giants, Borzois, Bodley Heads, Bollingens, Vikings, Bantams, Penguins . . . all looking up: "Okay, smart guy, now what?" Balzac looked up and said: "What do you want, tell me what kind of story you want and I'll write it, guaranteed." Meanwhile Pascal muttered: "Don't be a fool, let God into your heart." I couldn't take it anymore and came here, to you.

As usual it was three o'clock in the morning. Fortunately I was full of tuna fish, celery, lecinaise, pumpernickel, dates and coffee, so I wasn't going to kill myself. And after all these years I'm still here, looking for a story. This time it has another man and woman.

The man is at that round and even age of forty when everything will be okay. He's a painter. A house-painter and a masterpiece-painter, and he lives down and out somewhere like Spitalfields or Dorchester or any broken bottle factory poison dandelion sooty pigeon section of this great and tragic dung-heap, THE CITY. Or Fifth Street in West Berkeley, California. He lives alone in an old fat dilapidated balloon-frame house where the rent is very cheap and the people next door raise chickens and goats, and he's crazy, eccentric like a circle with a bump or a wobbly ball with a nipple.

The woman however is often a pain in the ass and odd and crooked at the age of thirty-one when nothing is ever right, and she's lonely as a frog in a bathtub. She works for the Post Office part-time collecting mail in her snazzy van three afternoons a week and all day Sunday, the rest of the time trying out therapies, Tai-Chiying, meditating, masturbating, drawing, crying, cooking . . . always looking for something, never satisfied, and usually going back to her piano, the vessel of her desires into which she pours her suffering and enthusiasm as if they were a diary of clouds, vanishing sounds that would be words rolling out the window of her gingerbread cottage to be heard or not to be heard by anyone or no one passing by.

The man's name is Harry, but the woman's name is uncertain. She always wants another one . . . Tangerine, Celerity, Welkin, Maelstrom, Sung, Palava . . . . Her real name is Nana but it's never enough. And her hair (as she looks in the mirror her hair always comes first) is also never absolute and perfect. Shoulder length and tawny with a dash of red, it's never full enough, and she's going to cut it one of these days even though she doesn't like her ears which are small but insipid. She's vain as hell and hates her nose which though not big is slightly out of line like porcelain that doesn't come out right. Her lips however are okay, good standard kissable sweetheart lips when she's in a good mood, and regular teeth with a sexy gap, lots of cavities but they don't show. But her eyes, her eyes are what she looks at when she wants to like herself, her eyes are what she wants her name to resemble, she loves her eyes, they are so dark and tragic, even though they cut like ammonia when she's in one of her pissy moods. Perhaps I should call her Dolores.

Harry could be called Pete or Joe or Izzy or Gus or any of those names that are like useful pieces of junk all over the universe, or like that hearty and omniscient creature: the cockroach. But Harry fits the best because it sounds like laughter. Cockroach Harry, the lunatic. There's a Turkish saying, *For the lunatic every day is a holiday.* And if one think not of those poor tormented people in laundramats and asylums, but of bums and geniuses, you can get a picture of Harry lost in a daisy or a chicken turd or whatever comes into his vision. Dolores is vain and specific and never leaves a pimple uncovered or unpopped. But Harry . . . Harry is amorphous, an enormous amoeba, just another blob, bald and innocuous like a dirty egg in the middle of the yard. The hair around his head is curly grey, the beard is negligible, the nose a little bulbous but unobtrusive, the lips thin but not tight since the mouth is usually slightly agape, the eyes small and liquid like pebbles under water, and the ears are flappy with succulent lobes. All in all he's not ugly but certainly not the kind of man Dolores would ever want to fall in love with. Especially with his hairless legs. One of the looks she can least tolerate in a man is a pair of white hairless legs. However, despite Harry's lumpiness, he is not a limp noodle. No, Harry has strength, and what's more, he is shiny. With his bald head and his hairless belly button he glows, he glimmers with a soft light like an overcast day when all the ferns and mushrooms in the forest are deeply clear and dewy luminous.

Okay, so now we have Harry and What's-Her-Name. And the narrator of this story of course is me. Who *me* I'm not sure, but certainly I am not *you*. And who you are is a big problem which I will have to deal with later.

Anyway, now we are four, Harry, Dolores, you and me, and the scene as we already know is in the city, and like all cities there is always a highway out to the "Country." Dolores would give almost anything to live out there, that promised land without streetlights, without sidewalks and diet-cola, without smog and cockroaches, without her bedroom walls that never sing . . . she would give anything except her loneliness, she can't give up her loneliness which keeps her here like a lasso. Melancholy on a hill in the middle of her collection route, the sun down and the smog a pretty orange, she looks out to the "Country," she and her loneliness, yearning, longing for a hairy husband, a baby, a simple life and a wilderness, a homestead with the Whole Earth Catalogue . . . she looks over the hills and imagines beautiful aspen quivering in the breeze, clean water and wild daffodils, a fireplace and a monthly royalty check . . . . Someday, she hopes, someday . . . . But me, I'm sick of that theme: "Let's go to the country, let's all go to the country, let's live like Ebineezer and Lulu in Oregon or Vermont or Wawa, let's go make Tibetan Sourdough Bread and tomato chutney like Scott Nearing and his wife . . . ." Well, go ahead, go live out there, Dolores, go piss under the fir trees and leave the city to the slobs, go ahead. But she doesn't, she stays in the city, at least for now, for after all she is my character, and she remembers that wherever she goes she is always human.

Harry however loves the city. Over here on the other side of the tracks, cozy in his house in the late afternoon with all the ants and the mice, he is eating oatmeal.

—You want some?

—No.

He doesn't ask twice, lowers his head and continues to slurp his dinner. Without any sugar or honey or yinny syrup! Not even butter or salt! Just plain gooey semen egg-mule oatmeal. Smiling!

—Oatmeal is wonderful.

He finishes the bowl and sits back and looks at his hands as if they just returned from a long vacation.

—I've been eating it now for thirty-eight years and it never tastes the same.

Dolores is not the right name. No, frying her vegetables, and not listening to the serious and monotonous news on the people-supported station, she's not Dolores. No, on clear crisp full moon evenings like this she's more like Michiko, which goes better with tofu and jicama on brown rice with green tea. On superb ceramic. In the zen kitchen of bamboo and coleas and kindergarten colors, yellow and blue and a careful red here and there . . . Ah, Michy, you got everything going for you, you got taste, you got looks, you got heart, you even got a little money. But you're so goddamn fussy, Jesus Christ, are you fussy! What was the matter with that guy at the party last night, what's his name . . . .

—Leo

—Yeah, Leo, what was the matter with Leo? He had a wonderful face and beautiful fingers and he wanted to have dinner with you tonight. Wouldn't it be more healthy, more Reichian if you were eating with him tonight instead of alone?

—He was too short.

—He was as tall as you are.

—That's too short.

—Ah, Michy . . . .

—Don't call me Michy!

I don't know what I'm going to do with her, I get so frustrated I want to slice her open from her neck to her vagina and hang her on a telephone pole. She's been sleeping in this bed alone for two years now and it feels like Emily Dickinson. I'm afraid she'll never get out. How she'll get together with Harry I don't know. Not that he gives a shit. To him she's just another beautiful woman. He's seen her around, lots of times. She's seen him too but never noticed of course. Once he was standing right in front of her in the Co-op. I told him to turn around and give her one of his shit-eating smiles and he did. But she couldn't see. Instead she was looking at some zenith of masculinity over in the corner buying imported beer. So now here she is in the middle of celery root and broccoli crying again, the same old crying, the cry of the ages rising from a deep well buried in an ancient land of misery and torture, a cry that trickles with a little giggle, then bubbles up, up, until she's so soaked with pain that I want to stab her right between her ribs. Help her, Harry, goddammit, don't just stand there with your fucking pencils!

But he doesn't give a shit. Over here with the AMTRAK rolling by his window, his bald head shiny under the warm lamp like an indecent exhibition, he sits at one of his tables entirely buried and lost in his own hands. And as he draws one and then other, (for Harry is ambidextrous), the lines swallow his eyes and he enters once again the jungle of serpents and creatures of prey. The undulating veins across the hatching of pores and tiny hairs develop into a protean swirl of slippery images that somehow always become snakes, heavy quiet boas curling over and over again like LSD hallucinations. His hands, his hands, his hands that did not belong to him but were his friends, his two *naga* buddies . . . .

—Rocco and Lefty.

He paid homage by drawing them over and over again each night after dinner lost in the mystery of their secrets, these hands that could create world after world like a dreaming god, their quiet fingers never ceasing to prey upon every form that could be seen or imagined, nothing was not food for their omnivorous writhing.

Harry jerks off, sleeps with anyone he can, draws his masterpieces, paints houses, eats oatmeal, urinates, defecates . . . all in the flow of slimy samsara. But Cynthia alone with her sex . . . well, I feel ashamed. She doesn't mind if I talk about her, as long as I don't do it like a liberated woman on the radio advertising a book about vibrators and new consciousness. Cynthia's not one of those. She's a pain in the ass and a snob, but she doesn't bullshit. So I have to be careful now as she lies in bed caressing herself, wanting to continue and yet knowing it will aggravate her loneliness. It was hygenic, vegetotherapeutic, and relaxing, it was okay, acceptable, common and natural, it was even interesting, but it was a poor substitute and never without shame and this moment of her life, the terror between shutting the lamp and falling asleep, had become the darkness she most feared. The details of her masturbation, what finger, what fantasy, what sound, what position she uses, or the history of it and how it began and developed and became the mortar of her character, are all irrelevant and just more bullshit adding to the libraries of bullshit about self-exploration. Only the darkness mattered and that there was only herself to hug and she herself was not enough. She turned, reached over and grabbed an armful of no one. She was thirty-one going on seventy and tomorrow she would die a moldy spinster, all her beautiful orgone energy gone to waste. She can't face it, buries her eyes in the pillow, and sometimes even tries to pray, *Please someone anything come and fill me with whatever it is that is not this shivering* . . . . But she knows that prayers are not for asking, and all she can do is watch her memories and hope they will be soothing. You can do more, my dear heart, but I will let you sleep now. Dear dear girl, you can cry, it's okay to cry now.

Noon the next day and Harry can't get his landscape right. The figures don't fit.
— Figures and landscape, that's too ambitious, Harry.
— It'll work out.
— But when? You don't have much time left. You'll die tomorrow and the Good Will will sell all this at ten cents apiece.
— What a bargain! A masterpiece for ten cents!
His eyeballs roll at the thought of an old Black lady buying one of his masterpieces in the Good Will, taking it home and hanging it in her kitchen, six nudes, trees, and rocks.
— She'll love it. Every day when she's lonely she'll look at my picture and I'll be with her. That's what art is, Sonny Boy.
— What old Black lady is going to buy a seven foot canvas full of genitals and hang it in her kitchen?
— You're right, it's too big. I'll cut a couple of feet off the side. Can't get that side right anyway.
He's so happy when he's thinking and his hands are sticky with paint. He was always like that, ever since he was a kid in love with Dutch Boy and the odor of linseed oil. The magic of the smear, the secret. He had always wanted to be that little blond kid with blue overalls up on a scaffold creating the universe, and now here he was: a success!

Mildred, too, feels good today. She woke with hatred seeping out of her nose and teeth, but then she vacuumed the house, ate both halves of the grapefruit, played Beethoven and Thelonius Monk, and then her friend Sally Moonrise dropped by and they drank French Roast on the back porch.

Mildred sat on the purple zafu and Sally sat on the brown one and they talked about people. Sally had met Lola Deertail who knew Mildred from the old SDS days and for the next two hours these two contemporary Americans, euphoric with caffeine, sat in the glass-covered fern and cactus porch and filled it with gossip . . . people, people, and more people . . . revolutionaries, jerks, cop-outs, gurus, phonies, vegetarians, entymologists, big shots . . . in Princeton, Boise,

Stutgart, Weehawken, Darjeeling, Mazatlan, Pittsburgh . . . there was no end to them . . . one person led to another until three o'clock and then Sally left and Mildred stared at the towhee on the plum branch across the yard. All those people, she ruminated, all those people. They were almost a family. But when she looked around at the end of ten years and into the quiet rooms, there was no one left. Where did she go wrong? First it was *art,* then it was *politics,* and then *therapy,* radical therapy, Gestalt therapy, Reichian therapy, and then *wisdom.* Taoist wisdom, Buddhist wisdom, Tantra wisdom . . . and still she was a mess. With just a little of the money she spent for all those trips she could have bought a harpsichord. Which is better, a harpsichord or a primal scream?

Meanwhile Harry is going full blast.

— Rhythm is everything. Time. Time is the Mother. Even the line and the dot are Time. And space of course is Time. All pain and all joy are Time. And Time is the Mother.

— Ah, common, Harry.

His eyes zip everywhere like two horseflies, hither and thither they go crazy with space until finally they land outside upon the robin on the garbage can, garbage can becoming grass, grass into tree, tree into jasmine bush, jasmine bush into more trees, streaky sky, old balloon-frame house, back to garbage can, grass and tree and Harry has another masterpiece! Everywhere he looks becomes a masterpiece! Even his own rich brown shit in the morning, even cigarette butts in a Greyhound Station urinal, even AJAX and General Motors, everything was food for another masterpiece.

But Jennifer doesn't go for that kind of stuff. For her it's not the swirl of fecundity that matters, but *design,* design is everything and everything must be in place and all men's legs have to be hairy unless they're Third World. Since she could first remember, her bed next to the bureau, bureau next to bookcase, bookcase leading to her sister's bedroom, the world revealed every item in it's place and if it weren't she would put it there and they better not be dusty either. She hated ugliness. There was no excuse for it. Someone crippled or maimed, that was suffering, that was not ugliness. But a booger dangling from your nostril, that was not tolerated. Nor all the other details in the galaxy that did not fit her taste, imitation Christmas trees, astroturf, the President's face, cigarettes, McDonald's, Las Vegas . . . were she Queen of life she would disintegrate them all with one of her teeth-grinding sneers. Instead, however, impotent and disgusted, she withdrew into her cottage, filled it like an antique shop, and buried herself with careful design. Her sanctuary. Her cocoon. She left it only at very regular times to perform very specific functions, like laundry and shopping, and now going to work. She walked like a drama, head high, back straight as if she were in a Samurai movie, down five blocks and over two to the Post Office annex. Up the dock, through the swing doors, slip timecard into slot, collect keys from clerk in cage, and out to snazzy half-ton, now no longer the cry of the ages but transformed into

The Postlady!

Always on time. Here she comes right-hand drive up the Avenue like Amelia Earhart, her hair in a snood, bellbottom corduroys tight and tough, hands calloused and heroic. Brake, stop, jump out, swing the great chain key (like bee-bop 1940's), flip open box, grab letters, shove in sack, slam lid closed, retrieve key, hop back in truck—Perfecto! All around the city she is the prima donna of the streets and everyone claps and shouts hoorah, for she is one of them, a mistress of communication, a sister of the tribe, a part of the cosmic design, not some pervert masturbating spinster eating lentil soup, not some pimple on the nose, no, now she is homo sapien first class, a potential Buddha! After her first swing she takes her break down in the lunch room of the Main Office. She sits back and bullthrows a little with whoever's down here. The lighting is like a Polish movie, the concession machines look like bummers, the walls are painted urine yellow and the tables feel like hepatitis, but the Post Office is not really ugly. It's banal, it has the imagination of a hamburger, it's as stupid as a congo eel, it's as sad as Wheeling, West Virginia, it's full of shell-shocked and demented clerks, but it's not ugly, and wherever she looked there was always a Ph.D. in medieval French, a sculptor of nylon, a Maoist, and all kinds of assorted bums, kooks and nouveau poor. And best of all the Post Office is 100% fucked up and inefficient which is the best design of all for a bureaucracy. So these two hours in the afternoon are actually pleasant. The rest of the day she can be Anna Karenina, but now she's at home in the world with her feet up on the chair and drinking hot chemicals and laughing with Jackpot the maintenance man. Jackpot says:
 —How's the new piana?
 —I didn't get it yet.
Jackpot likes her. He doesn't see any neurotic snob, he sees a good looking woman who likes to laugh and most of all who likes him, she likes him so he likes her. How could she help but like him, his old blackness and hard life shining like G major: *noble human being!* The Father she never had. With shiny hairless legs, no taller than herself, hot dog and mustard breath and body odor. Her friend. For fifteen minutes in the afternoon. Jackpot was good design. She could stamp him APPROVED.
 —Well, I got to mosey along.
 —So long Jackpot.
Well we're getting closer. If she can hug Jackpot and actually enjoy his odor then it'll be easier for her to fall in love with Harry.

On the radio the next day senators were interviewing the secretary of state about a world crisis. Harry listened with admiration and respect for these men of words. The different accents, the careful enunciation, the gravity and the wit, and the *importance* of what they were talking about—what drama! He was sitting in the toilet shitting and sketching a self-portrait from the big mirror opposite the bowl, the folds of his pants curling around his bare feet, hairless legs, and shiny kneecaps, while his elected representatives were fighting the bad guy. But like a true bad guy, the secretary of state was no slob, he came from Harvard, and Harry had faith in both the bad guy and the good guys, one way or another everybody would suffer but at least something was being done about it, intelligent men and women were debating and getting excited. What talent! What terrific vocabularies! The sketch turned out to be another masterpiece. And who would believe that one day an old Black lady would buy it in the Salvation Army for forty cents and take it home and hang it in her dining room: Harry's Self-Portrait, *Thursday Morning Bowel Movement*. That's humanity for you, capable of anything. Ah, Harry felt good this morning, the garbage men outside dumping garbage into their loud monstrosity, laughing and yelling, all the dogs barking and howling, an airplane thundering overhead, and Vivaldi on the radio while the congressional committee takes a time out . . . ah, the city is great, so much noise and action!

    —Harry, it's no joke, you know, the world crisis, important senators . . . .

    —I know, Sonny Boy, I know, that's why I have to keep on painting.

Meanwhile Bernadette was worrying about her car. But something was different this time, it seemed now that she was thirty-one and no longer twenty-nine she didn't worry in the same way.

    —You see, you have changed, there is hope.

    —Oh go away.

    —Okay I'll keep quiet. But do it right this time, think right. Remember the Buddha's motto is *Right Thinking*.

She didn't know whether to have her car fixed or not. She didn't need a car, but without one she would be one of those people who ride buses, who whenever there's a good time over the hills would need a ride, would have to *ask,* and asking for anything when you're over thirty is a questionable act. Time was running out, she had to decide, spend money or find a scam. The more she worried the more calories she lost, which was no good because she feels too skinny.

    —How many times I have to tell you you have a beautiful body? Right Thinking, Right Thinking!

    —Oh shut up.

If she had a car she would be mobile and independent like an adult. On the other hand if she didn't have a car she would be ecological and public. She decided not to decide and pay the difference (the fine to the Motor Vehicle Bureau).

An hour later, Harry was losing and gaining calories like crazy, drawing, drawing, eating dried figs and unsalted cashews, staring, drawing, laughing, pissing, drinking frozen orange juice, more figs and cashews, more staring, more laughing and drawing. always drawing . . . .

    —Harry! Harry, Harry!

You can't catch him when he's like this bouncing from point to line, line leading to line and back to point, dancing like the shiny green and black tail of the horny rooster, his bright red head pecking, always pecking, throbbing with a steady rhythm:

THE COCK!

When he's like this the entire organism of Harry the Painter becomes a giant penis fucking the world, orgasm flowing into his hands, drawing, drawing, drawing two pictures at a time one with each hand, his two snakes, Rocco and Lefty, Rocco drawing still-lifes and Lefty drawing landscapes. Outside, the chickens are burnt sienna and carmine against the deep vermillion of the grass. Inside, the pineapple, lemon, and avocado become an ancient temple amid Gamelon music. All forms swirl into each other and develop anew as he moves through a metamorphic jungle of grapefruit slivers and egg shells like so many clipper ships and icebergs. Sheets of newsprint, cardboard, paper towels, his weekly stash of cotton, bond, and rice paper, paper bags, old magazines, any paper that could be drawn upon, dropped to the floor one by one, first from Rocco and then from Lefty, each one wielding graphite and charcoal and pastel and brushes and pens of water-color and ink like the digital gestures of Indian dancers. Every room in the house had a stash of paper and jars of pencils, pens and brushes, so that whether he was eating or shitting he could keep drawing, and never was there a lack of something to draw, for wherever he looked life appeared, even the blank walls or the very air itself with its floating particles contained shapes that could be transformed onto paper. He'll be like this all day, dissolving his brains into an infinity of lines, and nothing will hold him down, for he is an artist, that hearty creature like the cockroach who never stops sticking his nose into every hole or crack that smells of life. Nothing matters now but that he keeps moving, that he keeps searching for the secret, that he plunges deeper into the jungle of the pineapple and the chickens and the refrigerator and the mirror and whatever could be seen or thought always, searching for the secret, the secret, that place where all forms become one, become empty. He's been looking ever since he could remember and he's never even gotten close.

Something happened to Brenda since she decided not to decide, it was like a miniature letting-go. Today, the temperature between fifty and sixty degrees and the barometer reading at forty percent, the weather slightly cloudy with a ten percent chance of rain, and the moon just past full with Mars close to Aldebaran and passing Pollux, Saturn, and Regulus, after years of rheumatism and headaches and fed up with her usual crap, she just let go and didn't care anymore about the car or her lentil soup or her manless bed. Instead she put all her concentration on dancing, dancing was her new thing. She could draw, she could play the piano, she could sew, she could throw, she could do anything with her hands, but now she was into dancing. Alone of course. Party dancing was too full of hustlers and liars. No, for now at least she would stick to her living room and her stereo and her music from India and Persia and the Jefferson Airplane. At first she was a little stiff. Being svelte . . . .

—You mean skinny.

—You're not skinny. Svelte, not skinny, *svelte*.

As I was saying, her body, willowy and svelte, at first found it difficult to fill her movements and make them round and buoyant like an elephant's, the animal whose dancing she most admired. But this very slimness became her best shot, because not having the opulent flesh of a sexy odalisque, she had to create it, to conjure volume out of space like a mime and let her breath inflate her body until it was almost floating. The years of Reichian beathing and kundalini breathing and meditation and tai-chi and health foods and misery and torture and failure were loosening her up, were stretching her sternocleidomastoidei, her masseters and the superficial abductors of her upper thighs which had always kept her legs pressed together. In other words she was losing her virginity. She was getting ready to be in love. Little did she know, however, who her beloved would be.

Late one afternoon, this future sweetheart and honeybunch, after another one of his orgies, did something he was very afraid of. He stopped. He lay down and sank into his emaciated sofa and closed his eyes. He was tired, and this giant penis slowly shrank into a little noodle. He closed his mouth and did not smile and let the low sun warm his face and curl him into a slurpy saliva nap, after which he would wake with spittle all over his shirt sleeve. But no, he does not sleep this time. Everything became blurry and golden and nowhere distinctive. He couldn't sleep, nor could he think. As he had before created worlds on paper, so too was he now in turn being drawn and swirled about as each breath became more and more shallow, each pulse fainter and fainter. He called upon his eyes and his two snake friends to lift him and drink some orange juice, but they did not obey. Slowly they retreated and returned inside him to coil and rest. He couldn't move. He couldn't even see. He felt paralyzed.

Well, we're almost there and my two characters are just about ready to get together and make a happy ending. And it will have to happen pretty soon or I'll run out of unemployment insurance. But how will they make it, in what laundramat or dentist's office will they finally meet and create orgasm? Millions try every day, fail miserably, become ill and kill themselves with a curse on their final breath for all happy endings. They do everything, they get jobs, they dress up, they buy cars, they go into therapy, they become therapists, they become pictures in Time Magazine, they write bestsellers, they win prizes, they do yoga, they run two miles a day, they even have children and pansies in the front yard and still they don't make the big time, don't get together for the really big bang. So then they get cancer and they die. And after so many failures who am I to write a happy ending? And yet I don't owe anyone any happy ending.

Harry couldn't draw anymore, and it was winter so there was no house-painting. Nor did he want to find other work. The weather had become his favorite skies and broken clouds, cold clean winds from Canada and the sycamore leaves dancing along the sidewalk. He tried to draw them, but he couldn't. Every day he would sit or stand with virgin paper, but nothing ever happened, until one day he didn't try anymore and left the house. He wandered. He took long walks around the museums and the galleries and the parks and all the streets of the city and at night he went to the movies. At first he carried a sketch pad and a pencil but after days of returning home with it empty he gave it up and left them home. Every morning when he woke he would whisper to his two snake-friends:

—Rocco? Lefty? Are you there?

But there was never any answer. And he would leave the house like a little boy on his way to school not caring whether he was late or not, taking the long way around the park by the water, not wanting to do anything but watch the seagulls. Every day for almost two weeks now the hills across the bay were clear and solid and the blue mountain rose above them like a mother. Everywhere became especially beautiful and when the plum trees began to kiss the air with their gentle blossoms he grew very sad like a Rembrandt or a Vermeer and found himself crying at odd moments, crying as if a goddess had just returned from a tragedy and held him in her arms and told him everything would be okay now. He was very tired.

One afternoon, on his way back from the museum, he was waiting for his train in the underground station, and the platform was crowded with expensive clothes and mustaches in the prime of life. He studied a man in a Bank of America suit eating a candy bar with the supreme confidence of an Achievement. He was a beautiful man, about his own age, with a briefcase and a haircut. Then at the man's feet, kneeling by the excellent shoes, Harry saw a leper without nose or lips. The Achievement did not see the leper, no one on the platform saw the leper crawling along the floor like a bacteria. They all stood perfectly alive and erect, waiting to go somewhere. But it was not the leper that concerned Harry, but the Achievement, it was the Achievement, the man of passion and a silk cravat, the chosen one, the tall stupid chunk of healthy and abundant life who now filled Harry's lungs with grief and love and suddenly he was crying again, overwhelmed by the massive ignorance of this paragon of evolution, and entering this magnificent creature he felt the waves of ignorance that filled every cell of his body, ignorance like a giant growth that would eventually swallow the briefcase and the haircut and the candy bar and reduce it all to even less than the leper whom nobody wanted to see. Never before did Harry feel so deeply the innocence of his fellow homo sapien and the ruthless stupidity of his blind annihilation. And he could do nothing about it. The great Achievement was doomed to his 5:20 train.

But Esther's been getting better. Her arms no longer ask what to do when she swings her pelvis, and her elbows lift like wings and expand her breasts as if she were proud of them. She claps her hands once in front of her face and once above her head, then clicks her thumbs and flips her head and kicks!

—Hadee Yalah!

—That a baby, Esther baby!

And she had bought another car, a Volvo! She was no longer a Volkswagon person, now she was a Volvo! At first she was not sure, the V.W. was so frugal and spare, and even the name of this new car sounded fat and excessive: VOL-VO, like a tuba. But then she realized she didn't want to be a bug anymore, she didn't want to be Mary Poppins anymore, no, now she would be a VOL-VO, a rusty ten-year-old one, but a VOL-VO nevertheless. And the daffodils were in bloom in her garden. Something was going to happen, she could feel it in her throat, something was coming and she wasn't going to wait for it anymore, no, alone or not alone she was going to do it, she was going to be happy, she was going to quit her job, get in her Volvo and go to Montana and climb the mountains, yes, she was going to get the hell out of her bedroom. She had decided last night lying awake listening to the caterwauling of the local alleycats. It got so loud and persistent that finally she had to get up and go outside and chase them away. It was almost dawn and she could see one of the old toms crouching by the blackberry bush waiting for her to go back inside. His right ear was bitten off and his face was bloody, and he was filthy with horsemanure from fighting in the garden, but he was defiant and would not give up and stared back at her as if she were the intruder in his life. He had lived in this neighborhood for many years now and she had always thought of him as a disgusting old lecher. But now, closer to him than she had ever been, the sky slowly become red and the light revealing him from under the bush, she felt moved and excited by his courage, by his bloody wound and the calm indifference of his mission. Who did she think she was, anyway, this fussy human, in her shivering nightgown standing in the frosty grass, trying to keep him from the big bang?

Like all geniuses Harry falls apart every so often and wants to die. He never did take that train but instead wandered back upstairs into the streetlights. Wherever he looked life appeared, the human swarm that did not stop, there was no end to them. All night he wandered through the teeming phenomena of all these little lives multiplying like stars, all their topless and bottomless neons glittering like stars. He would never be anything but human, there was no end to his life. Tomorrow he would be alive and, unable to draw, he would still have to keep living. If he weren't careful he would become like Van Gogh, eating paint and hating his friends. He walked until he missed his last train and then he hitch-hiked home with two kids who were just riding around looking for a good time.

And then one day when Harry was walking around the university he had to take a piss. He was right by the Student Center. And so coming out of the Men's Room, feeling relieved, he happened to pass the ride board, and there it was: that pretty little bird drawn with one of those new razor-point felt-tips. It was a copy from the T'zu Chow style (around 14th Cent.) and he stopped to admire it.

And then underneath it he read:

RIDER WANTED TO MONTANA
TO SHARE GAS & DRIVING
                    NANA 843-8506

And he suddenly felt an overpowering urge to go to Yellowstone and see Old Faithful shoot out of its hole like a giant orgasm from the bowels of the earth.

Yes, it was spring, and all her strawberry plants had little white blossoms. She was tired from being happy all day working in the garden, and so she was going to reward herself by going out to eat tonight. She was just about to step into the shower when the phone rang. A voice like Jimmy Durante's asked her if she were the Nana going to Montana, and she laughed. She told the voice that she would like to meet him first but that she was going out to eat in a little while.

—Oh, he said, where are you going to eat?
—At a Japanese place.
—Terrific, he said. I love Japanese food.

He was waiting for her on the corner and when she saw him she said to herself, *No, I'm not, no.* And this even after Harry trimmed his nose and ears, shaved close, wore his best sweatshirt and new pair of thongs and even brushed his teeth. But all she saw was *the face.* The kind of face she had ignored all her life and here it was confronting her with nine hundred miles and a night in a motel. A face like a tired monk waiting for enlightenment, a face like b flat: a wet noodle.

This however all changed the moment she walked up to him and said hello.

Instant Romance!

Shades of Loretta Young and Spencer Tracy, hot dog and sauerkraut, and the great goddess Uma coming on to Siva: *Oh my darling God let us marry for the sake of the universe!* I always wanted to be in love and here my characters are finally making it. She says:

—Hello, I'm Nana.

Perfect! Just right!

And he says:

—Hello, Nana.

But it's the way he says it, just like Jimmy Durante with his hat off. He looks at her with his wet matzohball face and says with tremendous orgone energy:

—I'm Harry.

She can't resist. This is Jackpot, Jimmy Durante, Akim Tamaroff, Johannes Brahms, Meher Baba, and Ali Akbar Khan all rolled into one.

Inside the Ozu Cafe the proprietor's little boy is doing his homework and watching *Startrek.* The proprietor, a tortured woman who is always smiling, bows and pours them tea. She draws the blinds but the sunset finds a few cracks and fills the joint with gold. Everything is perfect. Harry and Nana sit back and watch Mr. Spock and Mr. Kirk have an argument. The little boy looks exactly like an oriental cupid about to shoot them with patchouli oil and ginseng.

The tortured smiling woman returns.

—Some saki, please, Harry says as if he were President of Toyota.

Nana is very impressed. First he's Jimmy Durante and now he's the President of Toyota. She could have children with this guy. There's potential underneath that fat face.

But as the Buddha said, the end of living is dying and the end of every meeting is parting, and no movie lasts forever, a month, a year, at most two or seven, and then it's back to lentils and oatmeal. There will be good times, moments when they lie together in a tent and listen to the thunder and kiss each other like chipmunks, deep uroboric moments when they drive through the night reciting their autobiographies, great symphonic moments when they fuck like whales and lie sweaty and detumescent, glorious moments when they want all the world to feel their love, when they want to share it even with the shitheads, adamantine and shining moments when they meet each other in a crowd and hold hands of recognition, moments that will accumulate like beautiful coral, moments that will become like a life born from the sea, but all these moments will pass and they will separate and become driftwood in each other's memory and no love story is without death.

And yet, as they meet now for the first time across the tiny dish of pickled cabbage, even though Nana already sees the end of yet another love as it is just beginning to turn and swirl, even though she knows it's not forever and that she will feel that pain again when it is gone, she doesn't care, she wants it again, she wants it to grow inside her again, she wants this man, this funny man with juicy earlobes.

I look out the window now and realize I will never figure out the meaning of life, and the rose on my desk has opened too much and looks obscene like an ancient vulva that is much too sloppy. How will I ever manage the final orgasm of this love story?

—Make it witty and sell it to the *New Yorker,* my grandfather says.

Dead seventy years now he looks at me from the old brown photograph on my dictionary.

—I don't know how, Grandpa.

—You don't know how? You know how to write fifteen manila folders full of horseshit and you don't know how to write one little story that will sell?

—It takes a special knack.

—I'll knack your head off, knack, don't give me any knacks, sell something by May first or get a job.

His big Nietzsche mustache has no pity for my typewriter. His sons murdered, his daughters raped, his other grandchildren scattered across the desert, he scowls at my poverty and failure.

—Stop fooling around, sell something, find a woman and have children. Enough of this art crap, sitting here staring at the pigeons every day.

Do you think Tolstoi sat around all day staring at the pigeons? Are
you a writer or a pigeon-keeper?
— You dumb peasant, you think it's easy staring at pigeons all day trying
to figure out iambic pentameter?
But he's right. It's either publish or food stamps for the rest of my life. As my
mother was a seamstress so do I sit at this machine day by day like an immigrant
woman in a loud factory buried in dust and ephemeral fashion. I used to visit her
after school and hang around all those beautiful international ladies with their
stubby beards and aching backs. So too am I now a stubbly beard and an aching
back. We're all in the same boat and we all go to the same place.
But are Harry and Nana also doomed to another manila folder? Will no one
but an editor and an agent read my story? You don't answer of course because
you don't give a flying fuck whether I make a dust jacket or not . . . . I could get
sick again, smoke cigarettes and eat valium, and still you wouldn't care as long
as the pages get filled and stacked into layers like a compost heap for the garden
of my death . . . . You, you and your pigeons and your picture of Van Gogh with
his ear sliced off and your picture of Gauguin sucking his thumb and your
monkies from the Sung . . . . Always silent, never moved . . . thirty years now I've
been whispering to you since staring over the candles every Sunday morning
when you were just a crude imitation Mary in a dark and golden immigrant
church . . . my, how you've changed . . . and yet still the same old Fatso, the old
secret behind the altar, the frightening rats in the black crack underneath the
grimy boiler on my way to the garbage can, the thick green slimy river churning
whiskey bottles and swollen condoms by the abandoned barges on the
waterfront, the black slit inside the red and amber lights down in the cellar
where the slippery whore plays with her navel, or the hole in the clouds that
becomes a flower swallowing me into sweetness and perfume like a playground
swing with my legs up, the gentle daughter of the mountains, the giant madonna
of snowdrift and whirlpool, the old man of Stonehenge, the father of ele-
phants . . . . You, always you . . . in Ravenna and Texas, in a juniper tree above
the lake and in a tea shop in Seattle . . . . You that never left me even the three
times I almost killed myself, or the many many times I was so happy I didn't care
whether you were listening or not . . . . You now for the first time in my life a
spasm in my flesh like a wave of light . . . . You that lie buried in voices of silence
and are suddenly revealed for one quick look in the passing mirror I call
art . . . . You that crack my eyes with pain and fill my throat with vomit when I
have to eat my karma . . . . You beyond food stamps and failure, beyond lost
friends and a dead family, beyond the terror of voyages, you that live at the end
of all my bullshit, you that tolerate my bitterness and my bad jokes until I have to
swallow them like bile, you, always you, watching and waiting . . . .

All during the sukiyaki and norikabe Rocco and Lefty were writhing and
coiling, twisting pellucid noodles around the rice, throbbing with desire to reach
over the soy sauce and touch the beautiful woman with the bumpy nose like fine

celladon porcelain. Harry hadn't felt this excited since he first discovered Borobodur. After the fortune cookies the purple sky across the bay filled him with adventure and he wanted to ride across the bridge for a mocha-fudge ice-cream cone and lick it with her as they strolled around the fishing boats. She said:

—Okay, Harold.

And that was it. march 22, 1976, seven forty seven pee-em in the Ozu Cafe. No one had ever called him Harold before.

And so her chubby Volvo carried them into the jeweled city across the low tide of the full moon. *My darling Harold, my dearest.* She wanted to put her hand up his sweatshirt and tickle his nipples.

And so everything is going to be okay, food stamps or no food stamps. She will clean his house and burn incense and he will make her lasagna. He will be able to draw again and she'll play *My Favorite Things* while he does her portrait. They will live together four days a week and during the summer she will travel; they will miss each other deeply and when she returns she will sneak around the easel and hug him like a watermelon. They will lie in bed with their wrinkled genitals glued to each other like ancient pachyderms, and in the morning his warm and tender arm will feel like an elephant trunk across her bosom. He will draw her, paint her, sculpt her, again and again like a Degas dancer, never tired of her graceful precision, always turned on and amazed by the flight of her breasts and the wave of her buttocks. They will fight and discover each other's childhood and pain, but they'll never hit below the belt or elbow in the rib. They'll take long walks after dinner and watch the angel wings of the egret slowly lift above the mud as the great bird tucks in her long thin black legs, curls her neck and glides across the waves away away to the other shore. After a while they'll get a small bundle of a puppy, and after that they'll have a baby and then another baby. Their fucking will improve more and more until, when he is seventy and she is sixty-one, they will copulate like whales deep in the resounding abundance of their gigantic love. And then after both of the children have left home, they will save their money and give away all their possessions and go first to Chartres, and then to Saint Appolinaire, then to the Cheops pyramid at Giza, and then on through Baghdad into India to see the Great Lord at Elephanta. And death will not frighten them into old age. And they will die like Leonardo Da Vinci and Grandma Moses, wrinkled and writhing into the next life like natural childbirth. Nothing is not possible for these two wonderful characters who have suffered enough, everything works and anything goes as long as I'm here talking to you, trying over and over again, story after story, pigeons or no pigeons.

Stewart Florsheim

NIGHTS IN JAMMU

1

There is always this one thing
at stake:
a room,
shelter for silence;
a lover,
who keeps me
safe,
wanting.

2

A naked man, lying in a gutter, tries to move
from the path of a cow. The heat pins him
to the ground. He winces as he squirms to his left.

In a temple, a beggar shares a dry chapati
with monkeys. The air is filled: sour ghee;
curry; saffron.

3

For longing,
I go to a desert;
the sea:
I find stones
complicated
by stone.

4

In the Ganges, boys scream as they play tag
around the carcass of a cow. An old man,
mumbling a prayer, passes them. He stops,
treads water, looks up to the sky.

A leper waves his half arm in the air,
the hand of his good arm extends towards me.
It reaches my eyes and holds them . . .
a few paisa, sahib . . . ?

5

My eyes turn inward,
spooning light.
Hands
inside my body
ask for something
they have wanted to hold:
the stone;
the imperfect silence.

PREPARING FOR A DELUSION

Eyes that you gaze into, as if to impress
them with the urgency of a need, begin
to spin, to become the eyes of all the
women you wanted, until you see two stones
that reflect your eyes.

A mouth that you want to pry open, to
place words that you long to hear,
accepts you. Your tongue enters and burns.

You stop a woman to ask her a question
about how many men have wanted her. She
does not respond. Pieces of skin are grafted
over her ears. She hears you scream to
yourself that no, nothing can be terrifying
enough, as her eyes follow you down the
street.

NIGHT WIND

Like a woman
holding a man
she has always wanted,
for the first time,
the last,
the wave

does it slowly,
accepts the shimmer
of moon
and rises,

rises,
until the wave
stops being a wave,
the moon,
a moon

and the man,
moving away
from the woman,
turns his face
to her :
his light
in her eyes

Sarah Kirsch

SEVEN SKINS

The onion lies peeled white on the cold stove
It glows from its innermost skin the knife nearby
The onion alone the knife alone the housewife
Ran, crying, down the stairs that is how much the onion
Upset her or the position of the sun over
                the neighbor's house
If she doesn't come back if she doesn't come back soon
The man will find the onion tender and the knife stained

translated by Stewart Florsheim

SIEBEN HÄUTE

Die Zwiebel liegt weissgeschält auf dem kalten Herd
Sie leuchtet aus ihrer innersten Haut daneben das Messer
Die Zwiebel allein das Messer allein die Hausfrau
Lief weinend die Treppe hinab so hatte die Zwiebel
Ihr zugesetzt oder die Stellung der Sonne überm Nachbarhaus
Wenn sie nicht wiederkommt wenn sie nicht bald
Wiederkommt findet der Mann die Zwiebel sanft und
                das Messer beschlagen

Ann Woolfolk

MATINEE SYNDROME

There was a girl who thought herself pursued
by a big, black, frogman.
Dreamed she was whipped in the nude
by a svelte, mustachioed, beast of a man
who held a cigarette between his teeth
even when he kissed her.
She was a plain girl
simple like yourself.

THE WASHINGTON COLOR-SCHOOL PAINTER

By day he works as a butcher amid hanging hulks
his bald head bobbing and hairy arms sliding back and forth
dividing chops and lesser parts into neat parcels.
At night he chests his bag of goodclothes
and springs through the asbestos curtain that separates
his home from his shop.
He gets his ideas that way.
In his rooms again, his butcher's apron still on,
he pulls his colors from a deep sack
and sorts them into piles.
Then with his cleaver he knocks them to Kingdom Come.
They orbit for a while, until he calls them back
with painterly incantations.
He hangs them one by one over the door
and nobody gets them to move out of place anymore.

Frank Polite

HEARD IN A TOMB OUTSIDE OF EDEN

The way a poem takes off on its own,
you rise up every morning, mount your broom
and say "the forest needs tending"
and sweep out of the room just like that

as if you owned the forest.

The way you have of rummaging through
our wall locker selecting impossible tools
like jacksaws and chopping screws
and straws to blow a hole through holes and

through, as if an out really existed.

I mean, I don't know what's come over you.
The way a poem takes off on its own,
you refuse to listen to reason. You refuse
to accept that reason rules here,

that we're shut down beneath the seasons

for an indefinite stay. Death, dear Eve,
is simply the fact that we disobeyed in the
first place. I know what you're going
to say, that we must disobey death, also;

that we are meant to disobey.

I can't argue with you. I never could.
And it's true, I hate the logic of this box
more than I value any reasoned attitude.
The forest needs tending! The way a poem

takes off on its own, I'll go with you.

John Gardner

A WORD TO MY BLACK JUDGE BEFORE HE EATS ME

the White race is over
the curse is lifted
the prizes awarded
the gods collect their bets
the Devil's got somebody new to drink his beer
                              to drive his car
                              to draft his laws
                              to hate himself
the life he's got to hate to live
            to have to have and welcome to it
                        I can't do it animore   am
                        through with it   I hope you
    don't have to run so hard for so long with it   before you
                  drop among your crimes before your judge

Marina La Palma

WINTER IN AMERICA

Bread and saliva
sit in the cab with me.

It could be the wind
or the tangled crescendos of jazz—
nothing else is allowed or remembered.

Driving the truck like a knife,
I know this as a fat certainty,
the leaden taste that memories take on,
through my tight lips.

Water from the road above, where cars
are going the opposite way, slaps down.
I know it's "winter in America"
when History repeats itself into silence
and everything is flat, closed and definite

except for the hot smell of death
in the right-hand lane.

THIS CHILD

This child has no discipline, no rhythm
she plays chords that sprout wildflowers
            they mushroom
into more than she imagines

at night the piano purrs beneath her fingers

caricatures of faces
voice tones
these meager studies
light her way

This child has no discipline, no substance
her creations are of the utmost delicacy,
ephemera

Inside her mouth is a stone
thick, invisible and huge

her words are chained to this stone
(they can't squeeze past it)
her knuckles explore it with blind nudges

It's easy enough to say she should escape
it's easy enough to feel pity
but
that strength
sleeping in her
could devour continents,
nations,
thought itself.

Dorothy Wall

A room left
the light turned off
the gesture completed
and suddenly no remembrance of where it began.
Something flinches at the edge of vision
a memory of dark birds
a rush of hair.
The night air carries a smell
that can't be recalled.
The body is the same
yet always this shifting.

I need a place to be silent,
without thought
the center of a field
or a house on a country road.
A place where men stand in doorways
after supper and look at the sky
and women, watering in the last angled light,
pause and feel every night of their life
surrounding them,
where blackbirds on the telephone pole
are just blackbirds
and the stillness in the morning
is not frightening.

DRAFT

We stuffed paper in all the cracks
then old rags,
the wool rug.

Where have we come to
that precautions do not hold,
that even in light
your face is a confusion to me.

I cannot sense the direction of this wind
that flaps and drives against our house
like the things we deny inside ourselves.

ON THE BRIDGE

Quickly,
before thought,
hands act on their own.
Over the rail she throws it,
the past grown too heavy,
the burden, she throws it
and feels something open at her feet,
a round sawcut in the floor,
water beneath, blue and clear.
Quickly, she slips in, swims deep.
Small white fish brush around her,
leave flourescent moonmarks on her body.
She feels perfectly happy.
She will always be happy
if she doesn't look up
if she doesn't look back
at the bright pinhole above her
fixing in light the act,
the thought.

A woman stands in the open field.   The wind rises off
the sweet grass carrying a smell she loves and will always
remember.   A blackbird labors against the wind but no
forward motion.   She stops asking for reasons. At dusk
the corn will turn silver and all the sheaves will rattle
in place.   She will hear it as the release of breath long held.

Linda McCloud

THE HOUSE

the house. i approached in the fog along a brick path. enter through the iron gates. the doors are double off a long porch. the entry hall is bare except for one table with a candle burning & a note that reads your bed has been prepared. i walk up the stairs and down the hall to the third door on the left. the window looks out over the front garden. here too is a candle on a table and a bed the blankets drawn back the pillows puffed up. i blow out the candle remove my clothes and lie down between the sheets. it is black. as if i have not entered the room. i see a flame that has not yet gone out in my mind. i hear the scraping of branches against the house but remember no wind. a shutter clicks. muffled voices come from somewhere in the house. my mind is suspended above a black space. i feel it would be highly imprudent of me to move. when i awake the room is full of light. the window has been opened & i see the scraping tree but birds are the sound now some shrill and close others melodious and distant. i dress and sip the tea eat the toast left for me on the table. i listen for sounds in the house but hear nothing. i leave the room pull the door closed behind me. but no this cannot be. i open the door again. there is no room. a blank space. i walk down the stairs and at the bottom look up. nothing but grayness. i walk out the front doors close them open them, nothing no entry hall. i walk the path to the street blooming this morning with primroses & step through the iron gates. no garden. no house. i follow the brick walk that runs along the ivy colored walls but with each step what is behind vanishes into grayness. for a moment i rest on a bench to think over my problem. something is not right. the situation is unusual perhaps significant. to my right is the continuation of the street in bright sunlight, overlapping trees, red brick sidewalk and another bench barely discernible in the distance with what may be another figure on it. my meditations are interrupted by an old man who steps out of the gray fog on my left and sits on the bench. he tips his hat, rather weatherbeaten, a clean-shaven face with small lines of red veins, white sideburns, and a straight sharp nose. do you make anything of that i say pointing with my head to the left. anything of what he says. there is an arrogance about him i don't care for, a manner he has of holding his cane upright with both hands resting on the top. he's dapper i think except for the hat. can you make anything of the grayness i say. i mean you have just stepped out of it. i've done no such thing he says. i've come from the house just the other side of this wall. not a bit of fog this morning. do you mean to say that you saw no grayness that it's as clear where you came from as where you are going. absolutely he says. we sit in silence for a time before he rises and walks on farther and farther into the tunnel of green trees and red brick until he is a small blot in the color. he has approached the next bench and sat down next to what might be another figure. i am more confounded than before not only is the world disappearing on my left, evaporating as i traverse it, but the experience is happening only to me. perhaps i decide the man is not perceptive enough to have noticed. undoubtedly he goes on and on never re-opening doors never trying to relive experience. my meditations are again interrupted this time by an old woman who steps out of the grayness. she is far more to my liking: chubby, over-dressed, with rubber boots as if she is expecting puddles. she sits on my right puffing from the exertion of walking. what do you make of it i ask. what do i make of what she asks back. what do you make of the grayness, do you think it highly unusual. the grayness she says now where would that be. the grayness you have just come from, right there on our left. to our left she says is brick sidewalk, the street, a wall of ivy, and a house. i see only a grayness i confess. she sits silently for a moment. her cheeks have rouge on them and her lips are painted bright purple. the very same thing happened to my granddaughter as i remember she says. she couldn't remember anything past a certain point. amnesia you know. well we took her to a doctor and she got better as i remember, slowly, gradual you know, yes she got much better. but everything was a blank in her case she never mentioned grayness come to think. you're kind i say but my problem is different, perhaps unique, i'm quite confused. she pats my arm. don't let it get you down. why not look this way. she points to the right. lifts her heavy frame off the bench and shuffles along in her rubber boots down the street to what has to be the next bench and the next figure. well, there is no point in this i say suddenly in anger. i stand up and with surprising boldness stick my arm into the grayness and pull it back. it looks perfectly okay. i try to step into the grayness, but with each step i have misjudged my place and am still in the light. i try again. again. only after several efforts do i realize that i am several feet from the bench. the grayness is disappearing with every attempt. slowly i begin to walk towards the gray. the wall reappears. i am at the iron gate the primroses the house the fog coming in, a darkness, it is night again. in the entry hall is the candle, the note, up the stairs the room the bed the second candle the remaining flame the scraping branch the muffled voices, the blackness and my suspension. it is of no purpose i say to think about this.

Kathleen Raven

WE DROVE ALL NIGHT

we came at dawn to the high ridge
over Crescent City the sky was just then
deep green blue so trees stood out
in silhouettes elegant as monuments
two hundred feet two thousand years
against the backdrop of the sky and sea
and down the ridge we saw the lights
that glimmer in a crescent at the bayside
small buildings kneeling at the feet of rocks
braced against the winter sea

in Crescent City there is an all night restaurant
where an okie washes dishes with part of his ass exposed
because his pants are slipping down his hips
orange juice costs 35¢ and nobody tries to bullshit you
that it is fresh
like everything in Crescent City
it comes down the ridge in trucks
in cans and crates and packing boxes

NEW YORK IMPRESSIONS: 10.10.68

Portrait of Intent

I am a bar-
barian my teeth
are sharp my eyes
are yellow
And if by
God I had some sense
of humor
I'd eat ped-
estrians on the bloody run
from street
to subway tunnel.

Belden

FACE OF NO CURSE

(to carlos castenada)

to be among the first to lay hands on your books,
I became a raven and flew down the library chimney
                    hours before it opened.
but I had forgotten librarians also read:
only two remained on the shelves: IXTLAN in a sanskrit
        translation and A SEPARATE REALITY bound
        in a black cover embossed with FACE OF NO CURSE
                            in gold letters.
I like that title better.
it puts me in mind, carlos, of the story you told me
        about going to the cinema with your dog.
the man who chanced to sit beside you complained
        your dog growled and pawed him during the film.
but the dog was sitting quietly,
            having a fondness for charlie chaplin.
how could this man,
                    who could not see,
        know he was sitting on the seat of your ally?
the ally was furious when he returned from the pop-
                            corn stand.
the stranger was fortunate to get out alive.
and you, sly prankster, sneaking all three in on one
                                    ticket.

SURPRISE PARTY

I wear my viking helmet, the one with the curving
        horns, and a scottish kilt held on by a single
                            diaper pin.
when she opens the door I roar forward,
        ripping her blouse from her shoulders,
                        tearing her skirt from her hips,
        grabbing one foot in each hard hand.
"not tonight," she whispers,
"everyone's here, reading the will."
                        I look up

the relatives are sitting around the table,
                         their eyes are goldfish bowls.
the lawyer, bespectacled, dressed in black,
      holds the will in one hand like a paper airplane.
on the table lies the corpse,
                         a painted totem pole,
                    dressed for his wedding.
growling like a rabid wolf,
                         I plop her warm body
                    upon his cold one
         and toss my tartan over the lamp.
my phallus glows like a woodstove in the half light.
                              the relatives stare,
and I see them beginning to lick their lips
                    like expectant communicants.

THIEF

the final stairway leads to the wine cellar :
      dusty bottles filed on their sides,
      a few golden casks with wooden spigots.
as I take two bottles for my knapsack,
I see a basset hound watching me, her eyes
red as my mother's the day I stole her egg money.
I decide she will not bite or bark,
but when I push up the cellar door to escape
she rushes past me to the light and I hear the girl's
voice asking how her dog got out. I glimpse
the family standing in a square of lawn,
throwing and catching a blue ball with red stars.
      I creep across the cellar, jerk open the back
window, thrust my knapsack with its clinking bottles before me,
lift with my hands, work my head out—
      and see the ball rolling past the house corner.
the father, mother, small son and hound play
among the far trees bordering the lawn. the girl
runs up a hillock, her blue frock ruffling in the breeze,
                    a curving stick in one hand.
I freeze, willing invisibility,
                         but even as her head slowly
turns, surveying the estate,
                    I know she will see me,
                    I am thrall to my fear.

when her eyes meet mine I become a butterfly pinned
                                    by their beauty.
she calls to her father, points her stick at me.
I back into my chrysalis,
    pulling my knapsack with me, knowing
I shall have to replace two dustless
                                bottles
        on their shelf.

MAKING PROGRESS

   progress drove me in her school bus to the village
inn. she'd reserved a room overlooking the russian
   river. while she slips into a white negligee
I go to close the window and two
men, resembling laurel & hardy, step from the shrubbery,
                            beg me to hand over the tommygun.
   I'd forgotten it was in her violin case.
I slam the window in their faces.
  "be rid of it!" progress says, her voice
                        blue gravel sliding across the bed.
   I say the bastards might shoot us.
they burst in the front door, pawing at the gun, followed
by the inn manager, two waitresses, my sister mary — the line
                        extends all the way down the hall.
I slip the action onto single
   shot & begin dropping them like poleaxed cattle.
"I'd die before I killed anyone," mary says, cuddling
                        in bed with progress.
                        "I must protect us!" I say,
but I'm running short of ammo.

INDOOR PLANTS
(1 a.m. friday)

an avocado tree grows between our houses.
we've watched for months, waved, spoken once.
tonight she's naked,
   tending indoor plants.
green plants with purple stamens, red pistils.
her skin is strawberry in the lantern light,
   shadowed with heart-shaped leaves.

when she lifts the water jar her breasts bud :
   petals pierce my chest,
     my eyes drink belladonna.

she flows almost out of sight.
I creep into the bedroom, quiet
   not to wake my wife,
     raise the blind, peer
between the bare branches of the avocado.
thru the warp of her loom I see her kneeling
                 before clay pots.
mandrake blooms in my throat,
   I find my sprouting penis in my hand.

I dream of signaling, encountering.
the uprooted mandrake shrieks in my ears,
   flings off head's never.
when she returns for water
 I rush into the bathroom,
  snap on the light, wave,
   raise the window,
speak.
I am shaking like lilies in the rain.
the limbs of the avocado grow heavy,
   its fruits feel like flesh.

GREAT WALL OF CHINA

my parents had gone somewhere, I'm not
sure where. to america perhaps. a middle-
aged caucasian couple were caretaking the house.
he spoke excellent mandarin. in my parents'
house there are many children's toys and hanging
bassinets. when the child came and began pulling
everything down the caretakers seemed unconcerned,
I had to restrain his insistent *I-wants*.
   in my room I found all my make-up just
as I had left it, rows and rows of smooth bottles
and jars. I gave the woman the green and orange shades,
better for her skin than mine, in exchange for a shard
of mirror. when the rains came I saw my husband
splashing with the child in the water streaming
thru the narrow streets. I went down and put one
foot in, but it was chilly and I cannot swim.

Peter Holland

THE SOFT WEAPON

Come out fighting
or with your hands up or
run. For the living
there are choices, therefore
we wait. When I was small I wound myself
smaller to spring at a man bigger than I.
I wait, like a gun that's assembled itself
in ambush of a pass no one travels.

You can tell a hard weapon by its polish.

For the flimsy there are weapons of waiting.
Self Pity. Also
the love of weakness.
When I cry in my woman's comfort we are
horns made velvet by our skins, or,
coral reefs in a wave's commingling.
At any rate, not dead. Stretched out
we sway a little. Water is streaming. Vivid territories
of angel fish stream at the edges,
combat is entering the live current.
Where there was resting, there is a fist.
When the game is played, there is no trace of it.

Rachel Nahem

POEM

I am tired of hearing about the deaths of male poets
Villon, Rimbaud, the Cockettes
traders in cultural slaves
like ball teams, three French whores
for a Jewish virgin
Marlene Dietrich for a jar of your mother's tears
eclipsed   the sun of my beautiful body
in a time / space so far away
blotted out by the dark blood of oppression
I despair, I strain to feel its rays
is there a skin I can shed to get rid of this fear
this smell I leave everywhere for hunters
in a dark room I sift ghosts between my fingers
picture postcards of capitals of the heart
love that I gambled with is lost
lost, to the house that rigs the wheel
the wheel of memories that turns in my eyes
that stops at a number and can't go on
and can't go on
so must return, return to the fingers and toes
with which it all began
to the seven year old lying in bed
and longing for breasts on my flat chest
to the first feelings I ever swallowed
to the first man I ever tried to please
I'll live in a mud house without print or images
and when I come back there'll be no more ringing in my ears

Gus Gustafson

MUSE

Imagine a long counter cluttered with newsprint
something like a newsstand, only indoors.

Behind the counter a big boy
stands looking out.

He stands with his hands in his pockets
under an apron, a white cotton bib one.

Where the apron strings go around his back and tie in front
smudges show how he stands sometimes.

When the place is empty he stands around
like this. His hair is ragged in back.

He stands like this by the hour
staring out the big window.

Hardly anyone ever comes in. And you must
imagine that he has no idea of loneliness.

HUGO BOYSEN

In 1940
Hugo Boysen
ran the Standard station
on a corner of Highway 16
Murdo, South Dakota.

He banked
at the Jones County
Bank, bought Ball-Band shoes
from Gustafson's Department Store
had his cleaning done
in Presho.

Sometimes tourists
from the East asked him,
The wind always blow this way
out here ? Hugo'd look off across

the plains, shake his head : No,
sometimes it blows
the other way.

Hugo Boysen
was his name
for sure. The rest
might be mistaken.

Jennifer Stone

BEATIFIC BLUE

Late one morning in the San Francisco summer of '54, I walked to The Cafe of the Black Cat for breakfast. I was living in North Beach with a painter who didn't sleep with me. He couldn't sleep with me because I was twenty and that made me a minor. He had been in trouble once over a thing like that. I didn't mind because I had never properly slept with anyone up to that time and I didn't think I should start with him. He was probably queer and he had a tooth missing. He said he was having it fixed but he never did.

At The Cafe of the Black Cat, I ate rolls and drank chocolate with this actor I knew. We sat at a little round table inside The Gilded Cage. He told me to go to the Bella Union Theatre that afternoon and read for a play. He said he was sure I was just right for it. I was of course. It was by Shaw and the critic on The Chronicle called me a natural actress. Anyway, the play ran for six weeks. I stayed on with the painter and slept in the window seat and tried peyote and listened to a lot of writers and musicians and anarchists and actors too.

For the most part they talked crap. I don't think a person should take herself seriously unless she is alone. That goes for men too. I mean it's rude. These people hadn't figured out that nobody ever agrees with you completely, not really. Sometimes they would break down and cry over some issue or other. I was no intellectual so half the time I didn't understand what the hell they were getting so emotional about.

Once a woman got furious about some pictures in the painter's bathroom: some vaguely Asian prints of a fornicating couple. The woman in the picture was presenting herself to the man who was partially undressed and leaning on one elbow. There were these little flames all around their genitals. I thought the bland looks on their faces were supposed to be funny but the woman who got furious slammed out of the bathroom, gave the painter and his friends hell because she didn't think such pictures should be in the *bathroom* where people could look at them while defecating because that put sex in the toilet, lowered it to the level of a bodily function. One of the men said, well, eating was a bodily function and people weren't ashamed to be seen doing it at Ernie's for crissake and even paying for the privilege. The woman only got more upset and she said that was just crap. She just got madder and then she got stoned and went in the bathroom with one of the men. After awhile we heard them taking a shower together so I guess it was all right.

I wasn't so sure how I felt about all that bizarre stuff. Once I went to a party in a very modern old-fashioned apartment where all but a few of the people were naked. They were dancing and they looked kind of pathetic. They were good-looking, some of them, but there didn't seem to be any reason for their being so naked. None of the men had erections. There was a young guy dressed in shorts and a T-shirt sitting by the record player changing records. I saw he had braces on his legs and when he went out to the kitchen he was limping because one of his legs was longer or shorter, and so he wasn't naked. One of the women was curled up on the sofa with a silk scarf around her middle. She folded her arms around herself when she talked or laughed. When she got up to dance I saw her breasts were very small and she was very beautiful. I couldn't understand how she could be dancing like that in front of those men who hardly seemed to notice her.

The hostess was spectacular. She had exceptionally dramatic breasts and carried a tray of food around and leaned over everyone, asking them to try something. She was certainly old enough to be my mother and she asked why I was dressed. I told her I had spent half the afternoon dressing for this party, that blue was my color and besides I wanted to be different. Defensive as hell.

I went into the bedroom to escape from the naked lady old enough to be my mother and to fix my make-up. I saw the director of my play, my Shaw play, standing there talking to a woman. She was in the corner and he had his arm on her shoulder. He was coming on sort of strong and pressing against her. I thought she looked intimidated. I struck off a book of matches and dropped the flames into a wastebasket. She yelled "fire" and he turned around. I saw he had an erection but by the time he got the wastebasket into the bathroom and made the other people calm down, both the erection and the cornered girl had disappeared.

I sat down in the living room and began talking with a woman dressed in a wine-colored turban. She was sketching the nude figures. Bit baroque I thought but what did I know. She was drawing the dancing girl who still clutched her silk scarf. The words scrawled at the bottom of the sketch were "Death and the Maiden." I noticed the director come into the room with his clothes on. He came over to look at the drawings.

"People are not flowers or trees or temples," he said.

"You are," said the woman. "You're a liberal fig leaf if ever I saw one."

The director told me I was too young to be at this party and he would take me home. We went together to The Stone Pot for a drink.

The Stone Pot was in those days a very simple cheap bar and restaurant with the windows painted over and sawdust on the floor. There was soup and hot bread and mulled wine. It was on Montgomery Street just where it is now, but I felt as if it might be on the Left Bank and I might be the last of the Lost Generation. Everything suited my imagination except the people. I couldn't get them to fit. I thought being bohemian meant being yourself and I thought being yourself meant being happy. The stage was set but the actors had the wrong script. I expected to look up and see Gertrude Stein walk in with Alice. I didn't know Gertrude Stein had moved to Paris because it was *cheaper* than San Francisco. I was naive, even for twenty. I thought I was becoming myself and finding my milieu. I felt it was my "coming out" summer.

Chronologically speaking I think that was the same summer Sylvia Plath was in New York. Or hers was '53. Anyway it *was* the summer before our senior year, the summer she wrote about in *The Bell Jar*. She saw the dark side of the moon. I saw stars. I sat in Vesuvio's and I was the next great lady of the American theatre. How could I know I was Thumbelina without a tulip.

Anyway the director took me to The Stone Pot after the nude party. He was very paternal. I think he thought I had delusions of grandeur. He told me that the woman at the party, the artist, was a Lesbian and therefore a sort of psychological translation. Once removed. He seemed to be saying she wasn't up to the real thing.

After that evening he paid more attention to me. He noticed all the artifacts I had on my dressing table backstage and all my before-going-onstage rituals. Stanislavsky stuff. He said he hoped all the tokens and candles and dolls worked for me. I could tell he was touched. I had all the appearance and attributes of a precocious idiot child. Then one night an actor didn't show up and the director had to take his part. He came backstage to make up and watched me with my arms over my head, having my somewhat minimal breasts taped as high as they would go so they would bulge out of my costume. Then he watched me paint in a cleavage with greasepaint. He was impressed. I considered.

The Bella Union is a very old theatre, the oldest in town. I think it shows old movies now, or porno films. Anyway it dates back to the old Barbary Coast. There is almost no backstage area except in the basement. I had to exit by a fireman's pole down a spiral staircase to get offstage in a hurry. That night the director caught me coming down the pole. I decided he would do. I had half a summer left and the painter let another guy move into his place so it was pretty crowded. This director was rather old, forty or so, but a hipster and so forth. He had all kinds of appetite but only second-rate digestion. He also had a name but it's too biblical to mention. The first night we went to the Marin Woods. We stayed in a house with a lot of people and everybody slept with somebody so I think we went unnoticed. The next morning we had breakfast under great redwood trees and I remember taking careful mental notes of what I was wearing and what everyone said. I even wrote it down in a diary and saved it for years. Ten years later I threw it away. Secrets of the heart are seldom news. I mean he made love to me and I was very impressed of course with the idea of the whole thing, but I never had any orgasms with him. I didn't know how. I didn't know I had to get them for myself. I had been exposed to the women's magazines. I had the notion that orgasms were something a man was supposed to give you. Most men sure try, I'll say that much. They must read the same magazines. Or worse, they read D.H. Lawrence. I mean, when they just stop being in charge every minute, slow down now and then and stop performing, everything comes fine. Damn the finger-fucking fifties. Nearly ruined me. Men confused sex with athletics or with theatre, which is worse. It was all part of the phallocentric fallacy that men could do it for you. Live your life, pay your bills, give you babies, whatever. It was years before I found a man who let me come on my own, much less create my own.

Anyway, most nights after the show we would all go to The Other Place and drink. I was a liability. Not that anyone asked for my I.D. I looked decadent as hell in those days. I wore black leotards and mauve fingernail polish. I always left great smears of make up around my eyes. Kohl was advised by Colette. I read that Colette had gone into the cosmetics game at one time and in her pictures she looked like a zombie. So did I. Morticia Adams on the corner of Columbus and Kearney. Someone always gave me plenty of wine.

One night the director asked me what we were going to eat for breakfast. I told him I had two dollars and a pack of gum. Everyone got to talking about my going to an expensive girls' school and how I must be loaded or a debutante and I told them I was on a scholarship and didn't even have an allowance anymore. I told them how my father had found my diary in which I had wondered somewhat about my genetic prognosis. I was convinced he, my father, was in direct descent from Neanderthal man and not Cro-Magnon in the least. I had left the diary in a suitcase in my closet while I went away to act with a stock company the summer before. I never thought he'd read it. I just forgot to throw it away. Anyway, my father got very maudlin about the whole thing which surprised me. He was an M.D. He knew all adolescents hate their parents. Always. Anyway I had no money for breakfasts or anything else. The director was already paying child support and so he began to look at me with less enthusiasm. Of course I said I didn't think money was important. He laughed. He said I was a bourgeoise and couldn't help it. I said yes but I was a child of depression as well.

I went back to visit that bar last year, the place called The Other Place. I expected to see him sitting there under the naked light bulb. It's expensive as hell now, and full of hippie tourists, but he's still sitting there. He's the one with the grey hair, the sandals, and the Indian beads; the one with the young young woman with the long straight hair.

One morning there was an awful noise. The director's girl friend, his real girl friend, was throwing shoes at his door because I was in his bed. She lived in another apartment just up the stairs and I had stayed at her place a few times just after the play opened. She told me she was sick of him, that he was insincere and not the sort of man to be taken seriously. I had believed her because I didn't understand women. She had a charming apartment. She had it fixed arty and there was lots of sunlight and plants and bright paint. She had a bottle of Arpege in the icebox and flowers in the window and everything was clean and cared for. She used an English accent when she wore Arpege. She was a red-haired Jewish girl from New York. She let me sleep on her couch and gave me a quilt and two pillows when I stayed with her. She always loaned me a shortie nightgown. She would call in sick sometimes when she was sick of her job. She would say she wasn't feeling very bouncy or her cat died or something. I have tried to remember things he said that were charming but he didn't. He was too sure of himself.

After the shoe fight I took all the shoes back but I was too embarrassed to say anything. Worst of all, a friend of mine was sitting in her kitchen. Someone at the theatre had given him the address but he went to the wrong apartment. He was a homosexual who was in the plays at my school. He was always giving me good advice and he sent me a card on my opening night saying, "They loved you in Oakland." He had decided to look me up and when he found himself in the wrong apartment he also found an ally and asked her to rescue me. He was horrified at the garbage cans in the hall outside the apartment. Also the director kept his place rank and very dark. My friend came in but he wouldn't sit down. He stood around like the dean of my college saying stuff like remember who I was and what I represented. He said I better get my bourgeois butt out of there before the axe fell.

Well, I could see it wasn't Paris. I wasn't Picasso's mistress. I couldn't help believing it was bohemian and liberating even though I knew it probably wasn't going to be my "real" life. I saw something I thought was the new wave. I saw the ones later called the holy barbarians, the beatniks, the black and white, jazz and poetry, writing and retreating, talking and repeating beatniks. This was San Francisco anyway and I had come to town. My name was in the papers. I was appearing on the boards.

We used to see Mort Sahl at the old Hungry i. In those days the i was just across the street from the theatre and Mort Sahl would just be sitting at the end of the bar. He would read stuff from the newspapers and everyone would buy him a beer. He would start to talk and talk. Soon he had an act in the room with the brick wall. I could tell something was beginning. I knew we were all beginning and that was what mattered. I began to think I might be in love.

I went to visit the painter. I wanted to tell him I was in love. He was having a party and everyone brought something and cut it up and put it in a big frying pan and the painter stood there stirring. Now and then someone new would come and add something and he just stood there stirring. He told me he had thought about marrying me himself. He told me that was why he hadn't slept with me. He said he knew all along that I was a virgin and he could see now that I had no instinct at all for who had my best interests at heart. He told me I was making an awful mistake and wouldn't get married at all if I kept on the way I was. I got mad and said who was talking about getting *married* for crissake. I had to finish school, I had to go to the moon. I did not get through to him. I did not understand sexism. I mean I really thought I had the privileges of a white man until I was a white mother. That got through to me. I remember my father warned me. When I was sixteen my father told me to get married and then do what I liked. I told him we weren't living in the middle ages. He smiled.

I did get married once, a few years later. Me and Sylvia Plath. Same year I think. Then we had our babies. Same years. When her babies were still in cribs Sylvia decided to gas herself. I just left home. I put my kids in the car and moved back to town. I hadn't gone to the moon, only to Walnut Creek and back. It wasn't 1954 anymore. I remember I went to look for everyone sometime in 1966. There were some outlaws across town in the Haight-Ashbury. They were into color and flowers and sound. The black tights and loose words were all gone. No one wrote all over the menus, no one wrote on the tablecloth or the table or anywhere but in the toilets. They wrote alone.

I went back again to a place where The Blackjack Club used to be and I listened. I could hear the woman who used to sing "Little Girl Blue." She made everyone cry. It was a gay bar. I remember everyone cried. I remembered how she would imitate Marlene Dietrich with giant black fans and I remembered how I had loved her more than the man I was in love with.

Then I remembered what I had forgotten. I remembered a night at The House of India and a newspaperman I knew but didn't love until much later. He told me about myself. Some of it was true. First he gave me too many gimlets. I began to think the bartender was Trevor Howard. The waiters were students at U.C. Berkeley. They wore fezes and spoke in dialect. The man I didn't love yet told me all about being in love with love at my age. He told me Ingrid Bergman was my age or younger when she made *Casablanca*. I didn't believe him of course. He asked me why I thought my lover kept three oil paintings of himself on view in his apartment. Then he told me how it was that Ingrid Bergman was really in love with Sam, the piano player. I was in love with the song, he told me, and at my age he thought I should go back to school and act on my own stage.

Well, I never got much older. When I came back to town in 1966 I felt lonely. Perhaps I'd been lonely before, but it's easier to be lonely alone. There was chanting and feeling and psychedelic images and circles but I couldn't find anyone who would talk to me. They told me the Tao that is spoken is not Tao which is true unless you call it spoken Tao. I did not want to quibble as I could feel it was getting late in the age. Or I was getting there so late in my age that the words had lost their meaning and once you said them something died. Yes.

Anyway, I don't like to start getting sloppy and nostalgic. I mean to get to the end of my story. I fade into flashbacks and lying nostalgia because of course no one remembers right. Never exactly. I didn't develop the characters in my story. They were strangers really. I made them up then just as now. I never did find out who they really were.

One night I told the painter I was so much in love I wanted to get pregnant. I said then I would be taken seriously and claimed and loved. He said that was impossible. He acted as if vasectomies were a favor or something. Could be he's right. What did I know. I got dramatic, so I acted badly. Finally I threw up.

So about the ending. It never did. Oh, it stopped. It stopped when the director found a new virgin who was rehearsing for the next play. She was small and she had long dark hair. One night we were all drinking at The Other Place and he danced with her. When we got in his car to drive home he sat in the front seat with her and put his arm around her. I got bundled into the back seat with his red-headed girl friend and we went to an all-night party.

When school started in September I got a new part. Andromache in *The Trojan Women*. My acting teacher told me I was a symbol of all the matrons of Troy, of all the mothers of the world. I said I couldn't act in symbols. Well, she explained that the general or symbolic idea could be expressed or illustrated through the suffering of the particular individual, in this case Andromache. I took notes. She said I should act the role of a particular woman who has lost a specific husband, in this case Hector, as well as that of a particular mother whose son, in this case, Astyanax, has been slaughtered by the Greeks. I tried very hard to suffer. During rehearsals and performances I would go backstage and look at my face in the mirror and see the sweat pouring down. I was impressed with myself. I began to think I was suffering with magnitude. I thought about the baby I had lost and the heroic man I had loved and respected and who had died defending our home and our city. My ruined city. My Trojan home in flames.

One night an old art historian came backstage to see me. He had been on the faculty for more than twenty years. He looked at me and nodded awhile. Then he said, "You are not an actess yet."

I looked at him carefully. I understood this was to be taken as a compliment. I tried to look humble and wise at the same time and I asked, "What is it, do you think, will make me a real actress?"

"Time and the truth," he said.

The next night I was on stage watching old Troy burn and burn. The set was very impressive. I listened to the women screaming. Old Hecuba grey and granite in her agony. Cassandra gone mad because she knew and had always known. It began to get through to me. I wasn't tall enough to be a Trojan. I didn't know what it meant to lose a warrior husband or an infant son. On the other hand there was something about Andromache's suffering I could understand. I understood what it might mean to be taken across the sea to Greece, to live with aliens who thought I was a barbarian, and to be the slave of a man who didn't love me. I could get pretty upset about that. I realized I was pretty damned angry about my own fate. All things considered, I'd been badly treated. I was only twenty.

I went away to the seashore at Christmas. I didn't go with Agamemnon, I went with the art historian. He had an old place near Cannery Row in Monterey. He painted the same cypress tree every day and played old 78 records he kept in a closet. He drank too much and sometimes wandered off for hours but he looked at me as if he were seeing me for the first time each time. He was making a driftwood collage or montage or hell-of-a-mess as he called it. It took up most of the back porch and he worked on that some mornings while I tried to cook in the rusty kitchen.

Once he was painting the shore and I picked up a pile of kelp and began to drag it along the beach. He got upset and called out to me to leave it there at the tide's edge where I found it. Then he said it didn't matter. He put his paints down and walked down to the shoreline to meet me. I threw away the smelly pile of kelp and washed the iodine stink off my hands. We walked down the beach for a while. I sat down on some rusting wreckage and started picking at the sea lace growing in the tide pools. He found a horn of kelp and cut off the bulb at the end and blew a deep bass note through the heavy pulp. I began to hear the mermen. I laughed and he blew an even louder note. I was beginning to understand. Before

I went back for my last semester, I had loved another human being. I had loved someone who made broiled something for dinner each night and ate my breakfasts and who knew just how tall I was.

Bruce Hawkins

When God lit Adam's dreamy pilot light
he showed him for an instant eyes
which were the flat glowing bottoms
of half gallon jugs of cheap ruby port
tipped high, slowly receding. What Adam
saw next was the blinking rear end
of a long sinuous passenger train
disappearing at dusk around a bend
into a mountain pass. None of this
could have meaning to a man who hadn't
named things yet. It put him to sleep,
exactly as God had planned. Later God
hung around like some garrulous old novelist;
Adam, getting into naming things lost
most of his awe and most of his awareness.
This too, was part of the scheme of things.
Then all of that life was gone, Adam woke up
in the middle of the night, heavy,
with a taste of namelessness newly arisen.

AFTER READING CASTANEDA

I let my eyes cross
in front of the poem,
happens to have been
written by Alan Dugan,
and what do you know
in front of me now   ·
two poems have sprung up,
precisely as I
expected, both by
Alan Dugan, each equally
loaded with spite. I'm
not surprised, I'll just
read one and let the other
slip silently behind me.

But I can't choose which
and couldn't read either
if I tried, because
of the way they blend;

so I let words swim
and enter a train, stand
in the cold sway between
cars, gathering speed,
leaving town behind, sit
down and out the window
Alan Dugan is walking along.

A kid kicking stones, he
walks slowly yet keeps
pace with the train, and
the slower he walks the
faster the train roars
and they move together
through the landscape. He drags
his feet, wants to escape
into pure recalcitrant
backwardness: forget it.

So fast the train its
whistle is a shrill
echo, so slowly he walks
his shadow is thrown
ahead of him by
tomorrow's sunlight;
and he and the train
come in and out of
focus, giving me a glimpse
of drawn down grinning,
tight, spiteful, exact

and the red light is
my own nose, slowing
all three of us to a stop.
I have failed to understand.
It's like washcloths are
being wrung out inside my ears,
soapy tears trickle out,
enjoying this nastiness,
enjoying it, making
it up as I go
along, taking farms
at a stride; learning
how hard it is to read
or even find who
is where in one's head
with the eyes crossed.

FEAR OF SUCCESS

I become the road I travel on,
the moon that lights my way;
I come to a green which is the heaviest ecstasy.
If my muscles were this color
I could breathe underground,
I could wait on my knees all winter
here in this clearing,
pitch forward on my face
and let the strongest weeds entice me,
unsnarl me back through nature.

You come to an empty meadow.
The absense of wind is a shock,
it releases wild senses in you,
makes you watch for a voice
in the graceful bend of grass,
then whirl, ashamed,
toward the darker line of trees
which circle you like pen strokes,
suddenly closer than they'd seemed.

He sits beside me. He's my father.
He doesn't know it. No way he could.
He drives a truck, laughs hard, talks loud
simply my silent way of sitting hunched
is walls between us. He thinks I mock him
and if I tried to tell him I don't
the first slow unwindings of my tongue
would convince him I do, and the effort
would break up like a glob of mercury
under a thumb.
              He walks in
and sees two women flick a smoked off old man
out of consideration, and it's him they're doing it to
so he drinks enough to get up nerve to hopstagger over
and pinch out lecherously at one
and ends up on his face at their feet
and feels their laughter snubbed out in his back.

          He's one of these people

made an enemy of everything he never learned
and never learned anything
                    and so to protect himself
he makes the coffee take off like a jet in through
                    his mouth,
          he only has half a stomach
          but that doesn't stop him.
He slurps again
niagra falls,
and winks including everything
and starts in tellin' Katie here
she's a good old girl
but she oughta learn to drive a truck
cause she sure as shit can't make coffee

and I'm startled, looking over at him
to see the trouble moving in his face
all night past twenty four pump stations and motels
his grey belly drifting and piling in the wind
for no more reward than Nevada
                    and these fleeting thoughts
                    he sits with, staring

REGRESS REPORT

I think i'll buy a recycled pedia
it tells you everything in the world
that isn't a fact
it doesn't cost a thing
it's a truly reprehensive work

it allows you to study
the unrecorded media
everything you fear is there
and everything you hope for

some of the volumes are so quiet
it jacks your ears off
trying to hear

and if you don't like your ears jacked off
there's a volume quieter than sleep

the trouble is it's full of things
you'd like to hide from

the advisory council
advises
you only read it wearing tennis shoes
but i think i'll buy a recycled pedia anyway
if i can find the right repartment store

CITY OF PARIS

A cunt that smells like yank bubble gum ?
I know she's putting me on,
but she lets her mystery stretch
and pull tight each stride,
enclosing herself in odorous bubbles
of delight. In bubble

her eyes are lost, her head blown
all empty into a wishing penny heaven
but not ethereal, just nice and airy.
She looks to have inside connections
with the winds, incipient love groans surround her,
passing eyes catch fast in the sticky atmosphere.

White levis swell and seem to thin near
bursting as they strain to contain her busy and grand
central station and she turns the corner
to become a glutinous thirteen
year old cloud in my head.

I feel how she wakes
with the young dawn flattened on her teeth
and how she softly molds it from her,
carefully sticking her tongue through
and (gently not to break it) blows through rounded lips
then with transister intimately low and inches from her ear
enters in behind and wanders there from song to song
buying things she likes to have
while the pink foggy mirror swells
all around her, nobody quite touching
where it would break.

And the great god of bubbles, scarcely detected,
a slivery needle of San Francisco wind
squirms and skims through skirts up hems
down Grant Street with his fatal grin,
and she has been selected.

She ducks her head, she turns away,
she works her lips most lecherously
to keep it firm and rounded,
and the sweet pink film through which she glides
thrusts itself onward to its fate and begs
to be pricked where it is most protected.

BEHIND THOSE DARK GLASSES

hillsides are inching
toward the sea,
over the centuries
they rip fenceposts free;

we have graphs that
can prove it,
graphs so delicate
they measure

the breathing
of an empty street,
a skyscraper's
heartbeat.

———————

The joyous way a long string of words will glide in your ear
and vanish if you let it go,
across the path, open and shut—
to control it schools have been built
great universities constructed:
to step on a tail with explanation,
hold up a writhing prize
and slit it down the belly for our better inspection
until where skin was crawling
only anger and an itch remain:
only a terror of what might be forgotten
in the pressure of a crowded room
or in a solitary recognition
prove unknown.

THE SPIRIT OF PLACE

If so, I am an extension of rooms and lightbulbs,
strange neighbors and neighborly strangers
all themselves extensions of long interweaving strings
of vehicles through night landscapes. There is
in me an essence of the unusable space
which must by nature line both sides of highways,
railroad tracks. I embody the deep inner smell
of a procession of suitcases filling, emptying,
of silver lock clasps gleaming, springing open on
each new bed, of lids forced up in a small jump
from the coil of belongings pressed inside.
I am the product of a territory
which is formed at last from the unwillingness
to look any longer out the window of a car.

———————

Nobody speaks. We ride
along the bottom of this shade
peppered and continually slapped
lightly by sun and so always
half blinded, blinking, eyes
breathless and the play
of it tied in with the way
the car jounces along on

the dirt road. We are all
feeling deerlike inside
warm and mottled and
perfectly sunday, the beach
slipping toward us on the end
of a long hill suddenly snapped.

Still. Bright. I float. I
have an oddly watchful blindness.
I grapple back toward speckled silence,
toward carefully traced cracks
in time, toward
what ferns hide, glades hold.

SALT LAKE MIDNIGHT

We are a line
at gate five
moving our eyes
with mistrust always
to the right
or left of what
we recognize

in this indirect
light we wait
for the east
bound express
double decked
with pale razor
tinted windows
to remove us

one smooth thin
flowing shade

down the road
from all of this

uneasiness

It grows more difficult
to allow small pleasures
in myself, especially
the eyes which touch lightly
in and out of textures.

It grows harder to keep
from asking myself
what this laziness is
doing for me now, how it
is pointed toward survival.

Survival. Survival ! You are
a heavy boot all night
stomping back and forth,
all day leaving muddy tracks
between myself and the world.

At irregular but fixed
passages of measure, an
easy dapple of thought
and perception which is
the bearable face of time

returns to me. Out walking
the wall of a building
wood, brick, even stucco
gives forth silent ecstasy.
I move through autumn forests

each step shifting fallen leaves,
being altered in turn by
sunlight filtered through the trees.
But it grows more difficult
to accept this as enough.

A GREAT ANNELID WORM

has just crawled across
the tv screen of
every home in
the nation

a scorched ironing board
the picture
that goes along
with ringing in the ears

frantic citizens
begin to blink
at this
instantaneous fossil

but its nothing serious
a beer commercial
in ruins

momentarily
our reception
will be restored

on every channel
where the game was beginning
just after the shot of the billowing flag
this oily smear

much analysis
many metaphors
silent sets in living rooms
children wondering if they sting

wondering why we keep these things
issuing ghost grey light
or smudgy rainbows
and we tell them

of a golden age
a man of iron
a movie queen
a quarterback like god

ENVY

Envy, the small stone bird,
searches so busily
with sharp bird eyes
for the least flash of pride,
it puts flight out of mind.

It perches on wires,
whipped in the wind;
much of it enters the wires
until it is an even
smaller bird, harder stone.

The brilliance inside
the wires is never visible.
The bird grows older,
saddened with unfulfillment.

Like an old man
who has learned
the sewer system
of a hostile city by heart,
it walks in dark networks of wires.

That which is painstaking
has become so habitual
it seems carefree.
The bird, with its grasping claws,
wades among rats;

Its eyes have given up
their original reach,
the contours of its wings
have been molded
by a lifetime of tunneling

into the closed shape
of the tunnel, into
the shape of a sack

which is the bird's own body
which is stone
which the bird carries

through the tunnel
grown so small now
there is no room

to look down
at feet
which shuffle

in water which could be
lightning or lightning
which could be water

but which, however
you choose to see it,
becomes increasingly deeper

until the stone bird knows
if it gave up being stone
it would either

drown or burn or both.

REUBEN REUBEN

I think, for you, being dead
is just a different kind of afternoon;
a longer one, a slower one,
one where the sky drifts into salmon
and remains at just that moment,
one where the drops of sweat become pale
as powdery day moons on your brow
adding an almost invisible
layer of ease to the heat

and you lean back stretching and yawning
against the creaky lawn swing

one where you are always
letting the first notes of your rumbly song escape
while the pitcher of ice water
at your side stays cold and full

The cowpasture was one fenced block
thick and warm and yellow as
melted butter, where three fat cows
stood grazing among bees.
Then overnight it all went grey,
a carpet of dandelion skulls,
and the cows kept eating
with seed blowing fog around them to their knees.
And they were still there
when our car spattered past,
we could see them between the strokes of our
                windshield wipers,
munching lank grass out of puddles,
black and white splotches in the downpour,
overwhelmingly at home.

In the last moments
before its softness is gone,
when the stick you are writing with
moves more and more slowly,
the sidewalk smells
unbearably alive.

REMEMBERING IT

Remembering it
is creating
it again but

not the same
the same but
some lights turned out
but the same
but bare and flapping,
a shirt without
buttons, taken
from a grave :
both shining and faded
passing through
the hands that
reach for it.

When power fails the heart
grows stronger, the
swollen arteries of light
shrink back to size;
at dusk the continent
descends and streets and fields,
asleep, press loosely on through
space and feel
the stars : slow, strong,
steadily throbbing.

GAS HOUSE GANG

He follows boxscores
with his skin yellowed
and transparent between
the thumb and forefinger.
Where is Martin ? Collins ?
Where's the lip ? Where's Frisch ?
Where's Medwick ? The Dean
boys, where's the Dean boys ?
What is this trick ? He knows
how they are in this place,
how they hide his best slippers,
how they put wet on his clothes
to shame him. The world's a

mean place, meaner than those fans
in the outfield, in Detroit.
It takes a man like Pepper
Martin to face up to it.
The nurse tells him it is
nearing Christmas, she points
to a fake tree they have
rigged up at one end of the ward.
The lights are pretty, but
he won't succumb to them.
They have a new trick now,
they splash water in his face
until it feels like he is crying.

Laurel Taylor

AT THE BERKELEY DUMP
for Denny

Black men on the lip
of the gorge
tossing dead furniture.
Bone colored gulls dropping from
the sky their cry wet
inside of me the seasons
blood running on time
another twenty-eight
days you wading through
the debris of this civilization
looking for French doors.
Your lady is high above you
on a hill of dirt looking out
to sea.
The horizon is dark with trucks.

AT A HOCKEY GAME IN THE OAKLAND COLISEUM

There was always this dream of ice
and centaurs strutting and gliding
swinging young trees at each other
against the roaring dark.
So blinding was their beauty and
speed so fast, sometimes so fast we forgot
to fear.
It wasn't until they smiled at us
that we remembered that they had
no teeth, felt no pain, had mouths
vast and black gutted by fire could
eat us alive if we didn't
smile back.

We sisters lay still
beneath the surface
waiting
watching

their gleaming blades
skating
in patterns
across our eyes
frozen
open.

Greg Dunn

I CAN JUST SEE OL' HARRY TRUMAN

bangin' out a ragtime tune
                     on his nuclear piano
and sayin' t'isself : "Well,
if they won't listen t' Margaret,
goddamn 'em,
they'll listen t'me ! "

and Lyndon
at the movie house
pullin' a big ol' hawg hand
out of Lady Bird's sloppy crotch,
his eyes a'narrowin' to no-nonsense slits
as the first newsreel of the bomb comes on
   to a Sousa march

and 32-year-old Dick Nixon
in the South Pacific
watchin' the same newsreel,
blankfaced and rigid
in a crowd of cheering sailors :
                    His eyes adhere
to the shit filled bird,
they trace arcs in their sockets,
black suns crossing marble skies,
and his jaw falls slowly open
                  like a bomb bay
as the cloud rises over Hiroshima.

Ramsay Bell

ON READING KEATS IN A COFFEE SHOP

Startling,
the way men find me
"reading Keats," I tell them
asleep in a coffee shop.
Asleep to men
the way my thighs shift
with every new line
is striking, I think,
not thinking of the line:
"I feel them under me
like sea-shouldering whales."

Madeline T. Bass

THE SNOW QUEEN

This fair boy will satisfy
He loves me perfectly
I'll have him build
Air dreams and ice halls
I'll feed him creams with my white hands
He will sleep beside my cold canopy bed
Cradled, he will chant rhythms in his sleep
When he grows whiskers
I'll send him back to the little village
Mind wiped clear of all but
A frozen yearning
The memory of this beautiful figure floating
Beneath the surface of
His dark pond.

John Krich

ALL NIGHT LONG

from Frozen Man Speaks

The locker door banged shut, but it didn't stay shut. It didn't really need to be shut, seeing as there wasn't even a tadpole nearby, but Jack liked to hear the sound of the cruddy locker caroming against its own government issue tin. He liked this locker because he kept his work clothes in it. Changing each night into his Big Mac smock, Monkey Ward's gloves and Ben Davis grey jacket, made him feel good. It even made him feel kind of special, and Jack was as anonymous as his name on that big civil service list. Fucking safe civil service. Safe and sanitary civil service. Safe and sanitary fucking—he'd have to try that sometime.

Alone, all night long, with the humming flourescent and the puke stains rotted into the metal stairs, Jack was the third shift. "788 Days Without an Accident," the safety chart boasted. There were safety posters everywhere, on each and every pillar, exhorting Jack not to bump into himself, or skid across the work floor's emptiness, or tip himself into one of the few sullen canvas hampers. "Keep Your Eye on the Dog—He Has His Eyes on You!" A warning for the carriers who went out in the morning. Nobody had his eyes on Jack. P.O.D. labels reminded him that it was all federal property and all insured and all standardized and all shipped from one big warehouse someplace. Even the chairs had a patent. Even the fucking terlet seat had a number pasted on it. So did all those unused lockers next to his—a typical oversight by the overseers. Or could it be one day Jack would not be alone here? Sometimes it seemed wrong to be on this tour for all time; to have bothered growing up, to have eaten your Wheaties and gone to pep rallies and fought with your folks and hustled up an old lady and some kids, just to be alone like this. It was safe, it was good bucks, but it could turn you queer to the gills. But Jack figured you'd have to be a little queer to begin with for that to happen.

There were two deliveries a night. They were, colloquially speaking, a pain in the ain. You had to sort the sacks that came off the truck by their tags, get them on the right nutting truck, or dolly, then over to the right conveyor belt, or primary. Colloquially speaking, that is. Jack had it all worked out so that it didn't take him more than a few minutes each night. Even if he pretended he was one of those seven-foot Zulu basketball stars, and took a crazy hook-shot into the hampers with each package, it didn't take him long. There weren't no snoopervisors around anyhow. He was in charge of the fucking building, of the whole weekend parcel operation. The fucking fire department even had his name in case anything started spontaneously igniting itself. ("Matches Can't Take the Blame—So Look Out for the Flame!") All around the ceiling over the work floor were these walkways fitted with one-way mirrors so the postal inspectors could peep at you. But there were no peepers on Jack's shift. He didn't have to worry about the "sanctitty" of the mails. They could take their eight-cent titties and tuck 'em as far as he was concerned. What the higher-ups really wanted was for the bills to get through on time so people could keep coughing up the bucks. But no money came through here, just junk merchandise, the stuff suckers sent away for, or little gifties from far-off aunties, and nobody bothered to send the snoopers to look at that.

Jack found out on the very first night that he could read all the magazines he wanted. You had to snap off a metal band, then replace it later, but that was no sweat. "American Quick Service Report," or "Western Woodworking," or "Inhalation Therapy Digest," what did it matter? There was time to be killed. After the pay checks started coming in steady, Jack started taking mags into the terlet with him. The terlet was next to the swing room, and since there was no one around, he could leave the door open whilst he got in his cubby hole and sat. He'd take a shit if that was what he needed to do, or even if that wasn't what he needed to do, but he started to get hemorrhoids from forcing it. Then he started jacking-off. (Masturbation is much too long a word.) He didn't jerk it to the old lady, because with her it actually happened and that was no damn good to picture. So he used the mags. Even in the dreariest rag, you could find a Tampax ad, or some silky broad in a bathing suit selling Oldsmobiles or something, or showing off some foundation garment, or just standing there with nice gams in some pictorial section or other. It wasn't hard to stroke it and it didn't tire Jack out. That was the only trouble with this set-up; he was supposed to act tired all the time, but he wasn't. The boss didn't ask him to do too much, and his old lady treated him like some kind of invalid when he got back to the hacienda. No, she didn't ask him to do enough, not nearly enough, and he was bored to the gills with her. But who could turn down the chance to play sick?

From the terlet, it was easy enough to hear if one of the loads was pulling up, or if Al, the trucker on his run, was stopping to have his lunch in the swing room. Since it was easy enough to zip-up his Sta-Prests in time for any emergency, Jack started spending most of his time on the terlet. He liked spurting it out over the terlet seat, too. He liked dirtying the place, and a lot of times it made him feel special to leave the jism on the seat until it dried into a pattern over the U.S. government seals. He liked it when Al stopped to eat, even if he was a nigger. Sometimes, he brought his partner with him, an ugly Watusi prune named Eddie. Eddie had been in the Air Force a lot of years, so that one day he just switched over to "civilian" work. Got all his pensions transferred, too. Yeah, it was good and safe to work for the government. It wasn't like they'd be out on their buns if some clown at the top made some bad investments. Jack had the job for as long as there was a government and it looked like that was going to be for a very long time. A lot of long nights.

Jack figured out a rhythm so that the deliveries wouldn't interfere too much with his meat-beating sessions, but after a couple of years, especially after Eddie died, it got to be too regular. He'd done all the mags, so he started in on the packages. It was a bit rougher to deal with them. You were never exactly sure what was on the inside, and afterwards you had to patch it up, making the package look like it had been "Damaged in the Postal Service," not just ripped clean open. Jack's first success was with fruits and nuts. They had agricultural inspection tags on them whch made them easy to spot. But he figured there was only so much he could take from a basket of tangerines or a box of dried apricots before it would get too noticeable, so he slowed down on that. Besides, he didn't even like the stuff. Chomping on some health gourds by yourself while the flouro lights went on hissing over you just wasn't much of a kick. You couldn't measure out time with it, either—two apples per hour didn't make—so he had to find something else. He busted open some book shipments, looking for some stroke material, for the well-smudged pages, but he found mostly biology textbooks that didn't leave the imagination much leeway. He had his choice of the record club shipments, too, but wonder of wonders, that was no use. There wasn't no Jap stereo in the swing room. No, the P.O.D. didn't provide that.

Natch, Jack just started tearing into things at random. Electric blankets and chipped porcelain couldn't get too far from where he already was, but one time he got his meat-hooks into a shipment of lingerie from one of those Hollywood mail order places. All those filmy, pink, floor-length things looked real funny sweeping up the work room floor. They smelled funny, too. All perfumey like the box they came in. Jack figured if he could use a picture, he could use this stuff, too. It was a lot more like a real piece of tail than any picture. He jacked himself off holding some nightgowns, then smelling them, then draping them over the divider in the terlet. When it came time to re-pack the cargo, Jack kept one of the nighties as a souvenir. He stuck it in another locker. Now there were two lockers in use. At last, he had some kind of company.

It was fun for Jack to keep his eye out for clothing. After awhile, he'd saved up a real collection: a couple of titanic, quivering girdles, with all those flapping hooks and catches; a pair of correctional black shoes with thick heels; some sample throwaway paper undies; a one-hundred-per-cent-human-hair wig; and several packages of "nude" panty hose—just the word "nude" sent Jack to the terlet. He'd hold these items in front of himself, like he was dancing with 'em, or he'd sling them over the side of the cubicle and let them hang there for his inspection. There were so many combinations, Jack figured he'd run out of nights and retire before he'd tried them all. A couple of times, he used the whole set by pasting them up with the reinforced tape he was given to fix broken packages. The clothes made a nice, flattened lady for him. The hose hung where the legs should have gone, the panties at the crotch, all the way up to the wig that crowned the divider between one stall and the next. The divider didn't matter. Jack used both sides. Nobody was there to tell him otherwise.

Around the time Jack's career appointment came through, he started rubbing himself with the clothes. He'd just wrap any of them around his cock and use it to keep down the "friction." Sometimes it did get sore, but Jack still didn't get tired much. One of the panties felt so good on his cock that he had to put it on. It felt so good that Jack figured he might as well have it on all the time, under his coveralls. What were coveralls for? I put on my smock and my work gloves and my grey postal jacket each night, he told himself, so why can't I put these on, too? When you got in uniform, you were different. You weren't accountable. You weren't yourself. Nobody expected you to act like you did on the outside. You weren't getting paid to be that person. And the whole place suddenly belonged to Jack when he wore his new clothes. It had always been his place, but he'd never realized it. With the panties against his hard-workin' schlong, and the hose against his legs, and the girdle wrapping him up tight, and even the wig sometimes, it didn't seem to Jack like the work floor was the work floor anymore. The work floor was part of the terlet now, and the terlet was part of the swing room and it was all one big swing room now, no dividers, which meant the whole lousy parcel post annex was a locker room, his locker room. Jack liked locker rooms. He liked new uniforms. He liked to change. The only fella who saw him in his new outfit was Al, the old trucker, and he sure as fuck wasn't going to tell anyone. No, he wasn't going to make waves with the supervisors because of one white man's foolishness. They wouldn't have fired Jack anyway. His lonely name, alone in the night of lists beside a lonely number that mattered a great deal more than the name, protected him. A civil service job was a safe job—so civil, so polite. "Five Centuries Without An Accident!" Old Al just acted like he didn't notice. That was the great thing about working—nobody ever noticed, not even Jack.

Marcia Falk

WOMAN THROUGH THE WINDOW

For a year, she walked past my window
every morning singing
in the heat waves, in the rain
her basket of mint and parsley
balanced surely
on her thick black hair.
Her head straight,
her eyes forward,
her voice slipped quickly
around the corners,
and if she felt the weight
of her bundles
it showed only in the slope
of her breasts,
heavy beneath black linen.
Till one day this April
she stopped coming.

In the summer, the steaming Arab market,
draped with lines of carpets,
embroideries, old clothes,
will swarm with young Europeans.
Which one will soon be wearing
the darkly woven patterns
of her dress?

WAR IN EMEK REFAIM

On Yehoshua Bin-Nun, the eucalyptus are surrounding,
they've taken over the cypress and the clotheslines
and the bent roofs of Arab houses.
They've overgrown the horizon, in the distance
you can see the reckless swaying of their leaves—
silver swords in the wind.

. When the eucalyptus have conquered the streets,
we will edge sideways through the alleys

and grope along narrow pavements,
our backs pressed to stone and our hands
flailing at their resinous shields.

After us, they will take the sky.

Yehoshua Bin-Nun Street
Emek Refaim, Jerusalem

MODERN KABBALIST

You tug at words
like weeds,
severing stems from roots,
until your hands are lined
with graphic signs.

Then you come to my house,
your hands open
and dumb—
like the neighbor's cat,
proud
with its prey
at my door—
and scatter on my floor
a pile of thorns
in the shapes
of things.

What shall I do
with these
small
inviolate
knives
that scar the mind.

Peri Danton

LANDSCAPE

The border to the east
is a freeway
and to the west,
the bay and then the ocean
bounding on three sides
this American Carrara
a brickyard.
Except for the sea, the spray,
its sense of motion,
this landscape is perfect.
I measure my need for work
against the even piles,
the bench of torn wood,
the sound of
hammer, chisel, stone
splitting mortar from the bricks.
I trust the noise of freeways,
even the wreckage of steel,
twisted, frozen to the pavement,
the smell of gasoline
burning rubber, fitting
the bricks to their wooden support,
confirming their order,
the sound of
hammer, chisel, stone
repeated.
The sea is a nightmare
scattering the piles of brick
against their order,
throwing me back against
my childhood.
A pit mine would be better,
the tortured earth, a desert,
car tracks the color of rust.
I know the texture as dryness
conflicting with the bitterness
of gulls.

Chris Bahr

THE RIVER, THE SPRING, THE PAYOFF

Down in the pot holes you'd swear
those fish are tired of being fish.
There's not a smart one that'd figure better
to lie at the bottom and scoop up drowned bait.
With a weighted hook and a strong arm
you could pull them out by their heads.
Supper on the spot and they don't care.

Everyone knows now
there's no more gold in Snelling.
All those bald headed rocks
fighting off the spring grass.
Piles of old river bottom picked over
and left for miserable bugs and snakes,
left in the scorching heat,
glowing in the dark like alabaster skulls
mixed with the dry tiny skeletons.

River of dust, river of the brittle-legged insect
that scratches out its signature
on the coarse face of the land.
Tattered snakes
fighting their own dead skin
filling themselves with poison
staking a rock to die under.
Tarantulas migrating in the spring
creep down off the hills and wait in the road.
Half of them flattened, carried off by birds,
or swept down the road by the wind.
Remembering nothing,
they stumble over the twitching bodies,
there is no sign to stay in the hills from now on.

Get rich quick, a little blow-up,
sell the rocks to the landscape company
and get rich again.
Dynamiters and dredgers walking out
with the last bright flecks flashing from their boots.
Gold water, good as blood in Snelling,
sold on contract and no promise
that spring will not come like an angry storm
ending the desperate suicide of snakes.

Anthony Manousos

ARTEMISIA

(after a Dutch work by Gerrit von Honthorst— 1590-1656)

The scene is splendidly clear:
the widow raises to her lips the ruby chalice
wherein her husband's ashes have been mixed with wine,
and drinking it down, she sighs and murmurs through veiled tears:
"Now I'm your living tomb, my beloved."
In the wings the bearded courtiers gasp theatrically,
raising their hands, as if to say: "What a paragon!"
Of her attendants, one young woman with golden hair
seemed most impressed by this strange new cocktail,
(All this the Dutch master caught brilliantly,
nor could he forget to add, in the shadows of the curtains,
a crone with withered tits who can barely suppress a sneer.)

From far and wide, it's said that crowds of commoners came
to gape at this prodigy, the king's shapely urn.
Night falls; the widow aches. Her dreams
are like red curtains tossing in the wind.
Her straying hand has a will of its own,
    and it touches, it touches.
She bites her lips till blood comes and groans and sobs
and tries to imagine the king's face, a golden goblet,
tries to imagine the feel of his large rough hand
whose caress could be so gentle, yet set her a-blaze.
But now she can only see darkly
    too small red eyes like a rat's,
a sad mouth twisted into a sneer,
and an ancient woman's face
    peering out of her looking glass.

Ted Fleischman

HALF A BOTTLE OF CATSUP

I know.
I am sulking.
You know
what it seems to be.
A bottle of catsup
I am the catsup
across from you,
slouched on the front room sofa.
Aunt Martha's holy picture
smiles down on me.
But can I help it?

Please put me in the pantry.
Close the door.
I want to be left alone.

EMPTY BOTTLES

My wife is thin as reed stems.
Long fine hair, combs her hair
all the time.
My wife has small breasts. She keeps
one side of the bed. Nothing
I can do.

I wish all the time the knots
formed in the intersprings would untie.
Even though it's so late and dark
I wish I could bring back the bottles
for twenty cents each.

A crane fly crumbles its wings
against the air. Falls to my cupped hands,
won't leave.

IT WAS THEN

It was then.
Walls slanted
and termite work gangs
ate the floor.

I was left over.
I cannot forget
what I said to her.

I said there were
dark eels in me
and orange juice
cans. I said
my tongue was
a salty clam.

I cannot forget
her dress — flowers — skin,
caramel colored beer,
dust in the ocean,
the sun flat
on the bed.

HALL PASS

"Fortunate am I,"
I say to myself and,
"Quiet," or . . .
"Work," or . . .
"Get out of here,"
to the ears of the faces of
everybody else's children,
then send them into the office with exit visas.

Their stomachs gurgle on the way
passing Mr. Hansen's room
and my stomach gurgles too.

I don't expect anyone will ever give me my exit visa.

I think my soul is boiling away.
I feel it lifting on the wings
of a thousand moths,
their beady eyes pouring down like hail.

While I lay in the webbing of my hammock,
my mother rocking me
While I lay in the cradle,
my mother rocking me
While I slept,
my mother in my dreams
I kept all my mind on my toes.
I kept thinking of my feet
and how short my blanket was.

PRINCE POEM

By my bed was a long dull candle
as I thought of the princess . . .
like I, awake all night.

I thought of the golden pea
near her bosom
and how pleased she was in herself, as I . . .
yet glad she had not had to sleep
(through the long dull night)
on wrinkled nuts, as I.

THE TUBING PIER

In Oakland the south docks galvanized corrugated walls of the
storehouses of our cities and other cities commerce walls some spots
of rust, stand thirty or so feet above grey brown dirt and stones,
stand beside the rails of the railroad bed.

Today this evening I walk beside as the late sun beside the edge of
south dock and on broken concrete rock and wooden ties alongside
walk between warm touching the windows grit besmirched some-
times broken while the sun descends late evening sky.

I walk the bed while windows in storehouses watch toward the
tubing pier.

Dried grass yellow straws between the ties and thread to tie them
down paint them metal while they lie on their sides on wooden
beams straws tied at the tubing pier.

I have arrived to be here among you you great multitude of pipes and tubes so quietly lying for night and rest.

Hundreds of grey warm metal long bundles you and I, thousand tubes on wooden beams wait by tubing pier or harbor await the orange warm sun like I to melt with cotton grey horizon.

I would dream with you lie in dock on black rippling calmness or on gravel beds.

SPIRACLES

I went to her place at noon.
She was a petunia, my love,
yellow petals in my jaws.
I found I was eating her.
My mandibles
my maxillae
my labium
I was so happy
chewing,
I didn't notice
she was gone.

Even now I gaze
at the crusty soil.
Her roots still smell
of nectar and sap.

I might as well stuff glue
in my spiracles. I wish
someone would step on me.

Cockroach is nearest of kin to me.
Fellow dust kicker,
compatriot garbage eater,
we are all starved for sex.

Sometimes I look in your eyes
and there's compassion for me.
Do you want to hug me ?
Do you pity me too ?

Too bad things are the way they are.
If you had been prettier
we might have had a family.

Hooray
God save him
Silver spangled cowboy
who smiles at skeletons
who laughs at politicians
who has silver teeth and runs from nobody.

He was careless and lost
his money.
His chaps are dusty.
He jangles from the saddle
leaning far over and he's grinning
while his horse meanders
across the street.

When he died they put him in a box
and nailed it tight with sixty two-penny nails.
Lined it with pitch within and without
so he could float in the sea of the prairie.

I LOVE YOU RENO NEVADA

I love you Reno Nevada.
Yet you are too far away.
And do you miss me ?

If only we had some money,
we'd make a hot time tonight.
So what if somber mountains scowl.

It must be lonely for you.
Hailstones tumble down your boulevards

Scoundrels defame your comely virtues,
so now you cloak yourself in old lady's tweeds,
Southern Comfort bottles in your weeds.

Is there no heart in those cowboys?

Upon such a harsh hard world if you had a choice,
would you still be what you are?
Would you lie beneath a star
and hold up headlights' glare
saying, "I am Reno Nevada.
"Visit me. The world's biggest little city."

Lucille Day

AT POINT LOBOS

Four nuns flap on the beach
and squirrels eat from our hands.
The spindliest pines I've ever seen
grow here—a fore. t of bird legs.

On the bluffs the cypresses
pose like dancers. We face
the lavender sea, leaning backward.
Slowly, my limbs begin to twist.

A white-crowned sparrow lands
on my thigh. In future years
you might find me on a sea cliff
in wind, stiff, alive.

PATTERNS
For Liana, Almost Thirteen

A lacework of leaf shadows,
small flames of light
on a wall, patterns
changing and changing.
I wish all boundaries
could give way so easily
as I watch you struggling
into womanhood.

Did I ever tell you
that a woman is born twice,
that the first
person she gives birth to
is herself?

I have shown you all I know
of snow and summer,
of empty cups and the cellar
filled with wine,
of knives and fine silk
and dead trees and living.

I have pointed out Orion,
sword ferns, pines,
and red-winged blackbirds,
and held you close all night
beside the pivoting sea.

I reach for you now
but you burn
like a light too intense
to watch or hold.

I sit alone, but see
your face streaked with light
changing, faster and faster.
You, too, are alone
in a small boat
rowing. Push, push—
I'm waiting for you
and when you arrive I want
to be the first to know.

ASSERTION

Having listened
        to old men screech
        the tales of Wall Street,
        distant loins
        (the costly cuts)
        and other sorrows;
Having heard
        the young men moan
        for adventures
        in a coy cunt,
        citing grateful Bach
        and ballerinas leaping
        over Hiroshima;
Having received
        the meaning of
        a starved baboon
        chasing Eva Braun
        down Sunset Strip;
Having grown
        in the company
        of Bertrand Russell,

        the universal hero
        with his particular problem,
        Freud notwithstanding,
I am ready to talk back.

SONG OF THE STICKLEBACK

His belly undulates.
I am mesmerized
by its redness.

My own belly bulges,
ready to yield, shimmering
like the dusk sea.

My silver
calls him.   I arch my back
in a delicate posture.

He responds
with his zig-zag dance
and I follow

to the nest,
carefully placing my nose
inside. He prods

from behind, and the eggs slip—
so many pale jewels
beneath my fins.

Ragged and dull, ready
to drift alone, I leave him
guarding the nest.

Jim Tinen

HOMECOMING

I was in no hurry. The trip began
In rain that rippled down across the hills,
Tussled with the ocean, then followed me,
Lingering in the transient ivory blossoms
Of the apple trees, turning to grey sleet
In the mountains — then gone in the desert.
One day's drive across the sand and salt,
Another day's drive past hills and sagebrush,
Another stretched across an unvarying plain.
The land breaks like an ice-covered lake
After that, surging obesely into a rise,
Then melting into long, languid valleys,
Swirling and bouncing about in the hills of Iowa —
And settling down into the gentle ripples
Of the lean corn and black soil.
My mother weighed only ninety pounds
When I arrived. She'd rattle her hands
Against the stainless steel rails of the bed
And the nurse would bring the food or bedpan
The only things that she still needed.
Waiting by her bed each day was my brother.
He stayed all week, even brought his kids.
He watched her as if stares could cure,
A stare like a polar bear's watery gaze
At the tourists tossing peanuts at the zoo.
His children would stop their games of tag
From time to time, frightened by those eyes
Of LaSalle Street's best-liked lawyer.
It was awkward. We'd never talked much,
For we were each other's contradictions:
One loud, one quiet, not even looking alike,
One dark and lean, the other light and round.
He'd never even seen my wife and kids.
We talked of sports and storms and politics,
But it was when we got around to the family
That our conversation began to live.
We'd let each other in on family secrets,
Tell proud jokes about our old man,
Recall the fight to leave that home.

One day while talking of a crazy aunt
We laughed so loud the nurses were upset.
Then my brother heard his own laughter
Loud in the halls, silencing him instantly.
He looked at the floor for a while, and then spoke.
"You know how difficult the old man was—
Worse than difficult—we fought each day
When I was in high school, never forgiving.
The day we took him away to the hospital
I went to wheel him to the waiting car
And found him pondering the football letter
I won in school. He kept it all these years
And had to look at it in those minutes.
I guess there was left nothing on which to hold
Except the felt a substitute guard had earned.
And even so I'm sick and tired of her dying.
You say the right words once, and after that
You feel the words like dead frogs in your throat.
What can I say? Of course it's terrible,
But to me these words are like rhinestones."
Before dawn one day they found her dead.
The next few days seem flimsy in my memory:
Not knowing what to do with my hands
At the wake, while fish-faced people
Carefully walked by on the thick rug,
An uncle shouting in a flat voice at the funeral,
Concerning who sat where in whatever auto.
I left that night, avoiding all reminders
That the two who wanted my words were dead.
As the miles passed, I watched the grass
Turn brown and wither in the sand
Until the mountains, where the rain shook the pines
And ran in crystal wrinkles down the slopes.

Michael Helm

THE RECLUSE

At sixty-five he is a hunchback
still selling copies of the magazine from his knapsack.
All of his friends have become famous.

He peers from behind his bifocals
as his chin sweeps from side to side
tentatively measuring and sometimes smiling
at the involuntarily contorted faces within the passing crowd.
He is still partly convinced that perhaps one of them is planning
to kill him.
Yet another part chides from within
mocking his lifelong paranoia.

Banging his shin against a post
he stops for a moment to consider
the metaphysical implications of his position.
Perhaps with a little more vanity he would have been a success by now;
had published a book or two, performed on the circuit, and
been proclaimed at least the poet laureate of Alameda County.

Still, there is comfort   even freedom   in his anonymity
And the prospect of notoriety or acclaim appears a little unsettling.
Despite their frustration at his reticence, his famous friends
are secretly pleased that he, at least, continues to write.
After fifty years   maybe it's a sign
he enjoys the process, has an aptitude.
He smiles at them too, as if to say :
"To be admired
is not what I asked."

But they have thoughts of their own
and break into his house one afternoon while he is away
and photograph copies of all of his manuscripts,
then proudly arrange   with a librarian who is slightly deranged
for the posthumous publication of his collected works.

Enthused, the librarian hires a contingent of graduate students,
majoring in pastiche, to follow our poet and collect all his
paraphernalia — including any discarded napkins with
one liners on them. When it comes to success
one can never be too careful.

But our poet is not easily fooled.
        After sixty-five years he has learned a trick or two.
    He has the feeling of being watched   and broods
upon the meaning of the increasingly familiar faces.
In self-defense he takes to drawing ominous symbols; swords,
   daggers and skull bones laced with mustard
     on the napkins at the stands where he eats.

      Somehow that is not enough   and at night
he begins to recurrently dream of a rapidly expiring
and maniacal librarian who is plotting to kill him
and thus hasten the posthumous publication of his collected works.

The librarian feverishly whispers into his ear
over and over again, "there is so little time,
   there is so little time."

   This he endures until in one ominous installment
he sees a copy of his published book between two plates of caviar
containing all of his worst poems   and with a preface
written in heroic couplets by Truman Capote.

     He wakes up in a nervous sweat
   and begins sorting through his notebooks of poems
  taking out those he would like to forget.
    In the morning he carries the ashes out into the garden
     and buries them underneath one of the geraniums.
    But that is not all.
    He knows he must do more to protect himself.
Finally, after much deliberation, and with a supreme act of will
he sneaks down to the printer early one morning
with a copy of his finished manuscript in one hand
   and a gun in the other with which to consummate the deal.
     This time, he swears, he is going to have his way.

Unfortunately, as he opens the door and steps into the shop
there are already thirty-seven poets there
   All with bigger guns and shouting

     MeMeMeMeMeMeMeMeMeMeMe

In a rage he turns his facile, though long repressed,
tongue on them and with one scream
        scrambles their thymuses.
Intimidated, the printer gives him what he wants,
  even throws in a year's supply of sheepskin.
   As the printer begins work on the book
     our poet sits down to a meal of sweetbreads.

He does not feel bitter, even compliments his poetic peers
on their taste. When the printer is not looking
he slips momentarily down to the liquor store for some brew.
Upon returning he strips down to his socks and
chugalugs the three quarts he has bought.
When he is finished with this he burps   stretches   and yawns
then slides to the floor where he floats
into a dusty trail of stars inside the tunnel of sleep.

The next morning his sweet and languid memory is arrested
by a lady cop. He is charged with two counts of indecent exposure
in addition to publishing without any visible means of support.
But, at the trial, our poet is undismayed
and beams at the judge who in a jovial aside willingly confides
that after all there were mitigating circumstances:
The poet is old and has performed a valuable public service
with his recipe for sweetbreads.
The sentence is commuted and our bard is released
on his own recognizance.

Upon leaving the courthouse
he is met by a parade of well wishers and slapped on the back.
Invitations from the most exclusive circles
are stuffed into his pockets.
His family and possessions, he is told, have been moved
to a new estate patrolled by dobermans.
As he slips into the chauffeured limousine
our poet feels lonelier than ever.

That night, as he paces the cool marbled floor of the veranda,
he ponders what he will say
to the milkman whom he hears
is an aspiring, though neglected
artist.

THE PRISONER SPEAKS

We have been here for years.
In our quarters each impulse is registered,
There is a memory tape for every cell.
We are served lectures for breakfast.
All this is processed then promptly forgotten.
It is said an absent minded confessor
Is the brains of the outfit

And that he rides a straw horse.
For some reason he is afraid of what he knows.
Next week someone will start a petition
To fire him.
But we suspect that is not enough
And have conspired to wire the place from within
With an ancient juice.
At dawn each brick will melt into a warm loaf,
With our appetites we'll eat our way out.

DEPRESSION MAN

He sits there in his red leather chair, this man, resting with his eyes closed. His right arm lies by an ashtray full of crumpled cigarettes while his left brushes against the side of his bathing suit. Above his head, a thin layer of smoke drifts about the room with the help of the air conditioner.

Outside there is a swimming pool which no one is using. From its thin surface, imperceptible vapors rise. A dragon fly sleeps on a floating leaf.

The man thinks about taking a dip but he decides to wait. He thinks about getting up to pour himself a shot from the bar but he feels too weary. Instead, he remains at rest with his thinning legs stretched out over the hassock and waits for an impulse. In the foreground, the television is tediously droning

> . . . The National Safety Council predicts a record six hundred and seventy fatalities this Labor Day weekend. . .

Looking closer at this man one can see that his face is beaten by fatigue. It is pinpricked and slightly scarlet. This man's eyes remain closed and his thoughts drift back forty years to a boy of fourteen riding the freights during the depression. "Shit," he thinks to himself, "*Forty* years . . ."

Fourteen and riding a freight out of the South. "Sorry boy," an old familial voice croaks, "there isn't enough for you to eat here. You're going to have to make it on your own. Be out of here by the time I get up in the morning."

Or "Jeezus Christ, boy, you're lucky you didn't get yourself pinned under them wheels." Tough, whiskey breathed men riding the freights. Many stronger, more desperate than he. Others weaker, but full of cunning.

Like the snap of leather in air, a slow, thick-eyed yard bull screams, "Boy, when I catch you I'm gonna beat the shit outa you." The sheer malevolence of the voice, the eyes, makes him run faster, desperately trying to become a man. He runs as fast as he can, but sometimes he does not run fast enough. "Oh shit, please don't, god damn, please don't, please . . ." The rage, the anger, the shame. The weak do not survive.

Later, the summer and fall have disappeared and the boy rides west with the freights into New Mexico. There is a blizzard outside. He is cold and hungry. He wraps himself with old discarded newspapers for warmth. Their faded headlines read like a parody around his body: *BANKS CLOSED, RELIEF PROMISED, NRA PICKS BLUE EAGLE.*

> . . . Seasonally adjusted statistics from the Department of Labor indicate that unemployment rose 3/5 of 1% in August. President Nixon . . .

Meanwhile, the boy is freezing as the freight slows to a stop by a water tower. He slides open the door and walks out into the blizzard. Somehow it seems warmer. He walks along the tracks until he comes to the cattle cars. He sees the animals packed closely together, the steam coming from their nostrils and mouths. He climbs in to snuggle between their bodies for warmth. He has never felt so warm before.

The freight starts up again and the boy rides in the open cattle car, exposed to the flurries. The snow melts and freezes, melts and freezes in a hoary growth about his face. Soon there is a ring of ice around his collar and a torrent of sweat down his sides. His hair is matted with frost. He loses his hunger as the diesel drives into the white. He feels his body begin to feed on itself in a delirium of heat.

> . . .Temperatures soared to a record 115 degrees this afternoon in the Los Angeles Basin. Sun bathers are warned to avoid prolonged exposure to the sun for the next few days . . .

It is winter in Albuquerque as the freight shuttles into the yard. Winter and a blizzard, yet the thick-eyed bulls are as vicious as ever. A door slides open and the boy hears a man speak, "Shit, J.D., this fucker's frozen solid. A beatin' ain't gonna do him no good." Even in his delirium the boy can hear them, smell them. When it is safe he jumps out of the cattle car and screams at the pain in his feet. He cannot walk, or even move. His feet are frozen, bloated, cut by the hooves of the cattle. He crawls in his agony, his fever, his loneliness, not wanting to freeze or be found by the bulls.

Later, he wakes up on a cot. His feet are bandaged. Someone tells him that his feet were so swollen they had to cut off his shoes. But that is not all. With a start he realizes he cannot breathe. Two fists inside his lungs are squeezing him with every breath. It is called double pneumonia and he sweats and chills, sweats and chills. He does not quite know it, but he is learning a definition of manhood he will never forget; the weak do not survive, the weak do not survive.

Somehow the boy survives and wakes up a man at fifteen. He cannot remember ever having been another age. It is the Great Depression and he is a man at fifteen.

The weeks, the months, the years roll by and still it is the Great Depression. Men sell apples on street corners. Okies and drifters from the dustbowl of Oklahoma, Kansas, and Nebraska move in droves toward California for relief. Armed guards meet them at the border. Huey Long struts like the Kingfish in Louisiana. Roosevelt has his fireside chats. For ten years a job remains a phantom imprinted on men's minds. Work for a meal, hop a freight, stay in a CCC camp. This routine defines many men's lives.

Clouds pass over the swimming pool as the man changes positions in his chair. Bombs begin to explode in the back of his mind. It is the rumble which signifies the coming of war. Guns begin to be made and the jobs suddenly appear. The bitterness, the hatred, the neglect of ten long years are about to explode into a bloodbath.

> . . . Campbell's tomato soup is ummm hmmmm good . . .

Millions of men are summoned to fill the foxholes of war. But the young man has learned how to survive. He is fascinated by the power of airplanes. The adventure of aviation. Lindbergh is a hero to him. He studies navigation by day. Works as a soda jerk by night. In the process he adopts a young girl of sixteen for his wife. It pleases him to take care of her.

Soon he is the father of one child with another on the way. An opportunity to sit out the war in South America arrives and he takes it. He and his fellow employees talk about the German menace for the next three years while sipping drinks in the cabana between flights. The young man is a co-pilot, navigator flying D.C.3's over the Andes in South America. These are the glory days for the poor, white southern boy made good. Buenos Aires, Rio, Santiago, Lima, Quito . . . these are the glory cities with two inch steaks, ten pound lobsters, and the best bourbon money can buy. Eight hundred dollars a month, exchanged at twenty to one, is more than a man can spend in 1945.

> . . . you only go around once in life so you have to reach out for all the gusto you can get . . .

Two years pass and still nothing exists to be denied. One has only to ask; a vacation to Miami, a tour of the Amazon, a silver fox for his woman, money in the bank. One has only to ask.

Across the Atlantic, Germany collapses. Plans for the invasion of Japan are mapped. Military leaders speak of another three years of war and a million American casualities. Then, within the space of a week, Truman decides. Nagasaki and Hiroshima blow out like match sticks. With that kind of power, who can resist? Japan surrenders unconditionally. The boys come marching home.

Another year passes and the man takes a trip to Colorado. He decides to visit the father that disowned him at fourteen. It is now twenty years later, and the son returns with an attractive wife, two children, and a brand new Lincoln Continental. The old man seems shopworn and paltry by comparison. The son wonders why he has come back. Now there is only this gin drinking stranger in front of him, who has nothing to say. The family stays on a dude ranch for a week or two then heads back to South America.

Soon it is 1949 and the bubble is bursting. Bigger planes and fewer pilots are needed now. Navigators are at a discount, the army having trained thousands during the war. The D.C.3's get phased out and the 6's come in. The man is thirty-five and frightened for the first time in a long while. He packs his family and heads back to "The States," to California, land of opportunity. Meanwhile his southern brothers and the black man do the same.

And indeed, the boom is on. It is the beginning of the heyday for real estate promoters, aviation, Hollywood, and Ralph Williams. The booming Fifties. The San Fernando Valley awaits the buzzsaw of suburbia. But, for the moment, it is still a country populated by orange groves, eucalyptus, alfalfa fields, and horse ranches. There isn't a freeway to be seen anywhere. Ventura, Balboa, and Devonshire Boulevards are single lane arterials providing the only continuity for the whole valley.

Yes, it is 1950, and though times of prosperity are at hand, the man is unemployed. He has memories of ten years before and wonders what he would do if he couldn't ride the freights anymore. With a family it would be tougher.

But for now, he is an ex-flyboy with an eighth grade education and a bankroll. He thinks about what he would like to do. Sell insurance, Fuller Brush, a local franchise deal? No, none of these sound appealing. So he buys time with his bankroll.

He spends his time with pilots, actors, and other part-time employables. He likes to drink. His favorite place is the Hitching Post on Ventura Boulevard which opens at noon. Sometimes he brings his son or daughter along and buys them a Hopalong Cassidy or Shirley Temple. They even get to meet Hoot Gibson.

Somehow, the money does not go as far in the States. The cost of maintaining appearances goes up. A big home in the country, fancy automobile, lots of liquor. His bankroll is dwindling and over a few conversations in a bar or two he winds up in jukeboxes.

> . . . Show me that river . . . take me across . . . wash all my sins far away . . . While that lucky old sun has nothin to do . . . but roll around heaven all day . . .

It sounds like an easy set up. Buy nine or ten machines that earn ten bucks a day. Have a few drinks, shoot the shit with the customers, and give the owner forty percent. A nice way to clear four hundred a week. But someone forgot to tell him you need guns in this business. The toughest dives play the most music. Men with knives wait for him to collect from the machines. There are rumors of gangsters and protection rackets. His wife worries. It is no business for a family man.

He sells out at a loss and starts to pound the pavement with a smaller bankroll. He can't afford the bars any more. His family moves into a modest apartment, the Continental has to go. He watches Ed Sullivan and smokes three packs of Camels a day between shots of bourbon. Our dreamer is becoming proletarianized and he doesn't like it.

> . . . Harry, these sandwiches are delicious. Right, Sam, the Missus wraps 'em up in these plastic baggies . . .

The man thinks hard and decides that electronics, yes electronics, must be the answer. With a little practical experience he can bluff his way to the top. Any job will do for a start. All he needs is a beginning. Shit, thirty-five and to start at the beginning.

So he hires on as an hourly worker on a production line. Goes to work in a Ford with a lunch box. Bourbon in his coffee. He is part of the industrial army. He punches the clock.

People treat him like a liar or a braggart when he speaks of his life. Saying, "Okay, hot shot, what ya doin' here if you're so sharp." That stings. The man begins to doubt himself, becomes more defensive about his eighth grade education. He can see that a college degree isn't worth the paper it's printed on. But for him, it is an inaccessible union card designed to keep him in his place. He doesn't like his place and feels a mixture of envy and contempt for these junior eggheads. They should try the school of hard knocks some time.

Meanwhile, he stops drinking bourbon and moves to a cheaper blended whiskey. Hiram Walker is his brand. The Camels begin to get to him so he switches to the manliest filter tip he can find. Finally settles on Marlboro. He works hard. Twelve, fifteen hours a day. Plays politics for the job as foreman. He hates the politics.

> . . . Honey, I just got the promotion. Thanks to Compoz I didn't get upset at the meeting today . . .

The weak do not survive, the weak do not survive. He keeps telling himself that. If a man wants something badly enough he finds a way to get it. This man gets what he wants. First as a salaried foreman, back in the ranks of management—those in control—then as a technical representative with a salary, per diem, and an expense account. He treats himself and his wife to a weekend in Vegas. Blows a thousand dollars for the hell of it, then pays the finance company.

He has fought his way back up to where he can breathe. But it is exhausting. He is a forty year old man with an eighth grade education relying on common sense, experience, and the ability to act. He keeps telling himself that these must count for something. Yet, he sees so much pedigreed incompetence around him getting ahead that he feels threatened.

Beyond this, he is ironically an organization man now. Too old to quit, surrounded by politics, compromised by his retirement program. He hates the politics, the pressure. But one does not get ahead without pushing. He pushes.

He pushes too hard. It is 1960 and he suffers a stroke. A twenty thousand dollar a year man who wants to be president. He secretly wonders whether he has the energy, the stamina, the youth to go to the top. Perhaps his best days are behind him.

Yes, eight years an organization man and it seems an eternity. He has made a fantastic effort of will to get where he is. He feels he has nothing with which to continue his battle. Yet, he cannot relax. There are others behind him snapping at his feet, waiting to pull him down. He cannot allow himself the luxury of sentiment or emotion.

So, as if by another act of will, the stroke disappears. He tells everyone that it was a pinched nerve in his back. He carefully builds back the mask of invulnerability. He is not weak he keeps telling himself. The weak do not survive. If he builds the mask tightly enough, with enough determination, it will become a part of himself.

Now, it is 1960. The San Fernando Valley is unrecognizable. It hurts to look around. Ten years of money-hungry growth and the Valley is a wasteland of concrete freeways, apartment houses, box dwellings, and smog. There are two million people living there now. Ralph Williams and Harry Vonzell must have sold almost everyone a used car or second mortgage.

... For only $49.50 a month you too can have a secluded piece of waterfront property, scented by pines, on Lake Havasu. Call Exeter 4-7315 now for further ...

Nineteen-Sixty and still fighting a thirty year war. The man gets up every morning at five-thirty. Goes into the kitchen to pour himself a shot. Follows that with a cup of coffee, then another shot. In between, he smokes three cigarettes and talks to his dog who is loyal and eager to please. He does this every morning before going to work.

The man drives a Chevrolet now. But he still thinks of the Continental. He pilots the car like an airplane. Checks all the gauges: oil, gas, generator. Doors locked, tires firm, emergency brake off. He lets the engine idle until it is warm. Then, finally, procedurally satisfied, pulls out on to the asphalt street and heads east across the Valley to Burbank.

It is 1962 and the man has two kids in college. He still thinks of them as kids. He is suspicious of college and what it represents. Particularly suspicious of Liberal Arts. He urges something practical. Business, Science, or Mathematics. But the social pot of the Sixties is brewing and he is politely ignored. He recognizes that a degree in P.E. is as good as any, so he gives in. "All right," he grudgingly relents, "major in Liberal Arts, but don't believe any of it."

This does not work. The colleges are full of professional saviors, bleeding hearts. His children are youthful and idealistic. Changes begin to take place and the man becomes enraged. Snot nosed kids and a bunch of eggheads are going to tell him how to solve the world's problems? "Bullshit." Love your fellow man? "That and a dime will get you a cup of coffee." He does not believe in something for nothing. He has always paid, why shouldn't they? Men are not victims of their environment. It is an argument for the weak and the lazy. Let them get out and struggle as he has struggled.

... When a man has worked hard he deserves to settle back and enjoy a nice cool burgie ...

The children are tired of being children. Tired of listening to the voice of someone else's experience. They move out. A few years go by and the conversations practically cease. When visiting, the television holds them together. The children have a degree, a union card, but no communication and the jobs seem hardly worth having.

A political malaise descends upon America. The man feels older and does not understand it. ASSASSINATIONS, WAR, RACE RIOTS. His youngest son lets his hair grow long, gets spaced out on drugs. The man's whole world is collapsing. Queer, long-haired freaks mouthing peace, niggers rioting, screaming, "We're gonna get yuh whitey." Pampered kids playing poor on welfare and food stamps. "This shit has got to stop," he thinks. "God damn it, this shit has got to stop."

... Charges were today pressed against seven radicals prominent in the riots during the Democratic National Convention last week.

"Draft the punks," he fumes. "Beat a few heads . . . Teach them the school of hard knocks." But the confrontation accelerates. Berkeley, Santa Barbara fall under seige. Ronald Reagan becomes a leading man riding the horse of authority.

> . . . Miners in Death Valley Days would have loved to use Twenty Mule Team Borax to keep clean with . . .

"That's right, clean it up." "Clean the whole fucking mess up." "Cut their hair and give them a bath." "If they don't listen then shoot them." Blood spurts from the barrels of guns in Ohio, Mississippi, California, South Carolina. It is the late Sixties and the man has been drinking too much, smoking too much, getting angry too often. "Fuck 'em," he thinks. "It's their world now. They'll learn, they'll find out it isn't so easy. Then let them ask about the brotherhood of mankind."

Still, the man is not reconciled. His anger infuriates him. He drinks to dull his anger. But the whiskey just doesn't taste good anymore, his cigarettes don't taste good anymore, nothing tastes good anymore. He gets drunk quicker, coughs all the time. There must be a better way, he thinks. But he doesn't have any energy with which to begin something new.

He contemplates retirement. Sitting out along the beach in Mexico or Hawaii, letting the warm bourboned sun caress his body. He wonders if he has the stamina to make it four more years to retirement. Four more years and he can say, "Fuck it." He can wander off to the beach. Bake his bones to ease the weariness. Four more years.

Outside the sun is lazily setting, illuminating a crimson horizon. The man gets up, walks out, and dives into the pool. His momentum carries him forward. Like a blind man, or a child, he momentarily reaches out with his extended arms. For a suspended second or two he relaxes with the total ease of acceptance, with total surrender. Then his hands touch concrete on the other side.

In a moment he is sitting on the ledge, his distended feet dangling in the water. The ripples gently lap at his calves. Slowly he feels the heat building back into his body. The chlorine teases his eyes. Then, subtly, the water becomes perfectly still, as if no one has ever been there. The stillness and silence sing sweetly to the man until he remembers he is angry.

A dragon fly circles once, twice around the pool, like an insult, then settles. The man pulls his bleached legs out of the water and walks dripping over to a striped basketball. Red, white, and blue, it rests by a cactus plant. He bends over, lifts it up carefully past his paunch. Then when he is ready rifles it into the center of the pool. As if exploded by the shot, the dragonfly starts, up over the house . . . hovers momentarily . . . crazy . . . then is gone.

Mary Lane

THE GOOD NEWS
FROM THE FORSYTHE DENTAL CLINIC

My body . . .

They are young, fresh-cheeked, white-capped,
mini-skirted, they swirl, they stand,
each over her own chair
bending into her patient's mouth. Mine
sits on a stool, sharp probe
in her hand, she scrapes,
she has been scraping
calculus, plaque when it's hardened, old,
turned into bone,
she is scraping my teeth.
My body, old, thick, heavy,
lies on the chair,
stomach, thighs, nothing
about me is beautiful,
how did my teeth get so bad?
There are cavities, too,
next we will see the holes,
they will work on my teeth for days,
an hour she has been scraping,
she's worked her way almost around,
she's still on the bottom,
there are teeth on the top—
she will work for years in her white skirt,
young fresh face making
me perfect,
no one before her
has taken my teeth so seriously.

And what of my legs, my arms, my muscles,
my bones, my kidneys, my lungs, I have so many parts,
they are used, many things
have passed through, I have been away
from these white-faced girls with their starched white caps.
On the questionnaire
I have answered the questions,
'Check yes or no: syphilis, typhus, tb,
cancer, weakness of spirit,

migraine, depression,
mumps, and the pox.'
Yes, I said, yes, I have known these,
and the white-clad angels wear rubber gloves
like the doctor wears to touch my insides,
my holy ugly places—gums? did you ever see gums,
holding your fingers inside your lips and spreading them?

None of these things I say are things that you could not say—
as I walked in the sun, I knew
what I felt
comes again and again . . .
When she finally stopped scraping
I asked her who was to blame for that hardened plaque,
me or the dentists who hadn't scraped,
and she was not concerned with blame.
She told me the dangers—
under the gums, it loosens
teeth, and they fall—
then she said, 'Once it is off,
you can prevent it from coming again:
brush, and use floss.
We have made your teeth pure
again, you can keep
your teeth.'

The blessing, forgiveness and blessing,
I am clean—
not 'I', only my teeth,
but this is a start, this a beginning.
They send me out on the street with the promise
that if I use floss I can move, forward,
into the world, keeping my teeth
as pure as they can be, considering
that I will use them,
that I am human,
that I live in the world.

David Lampert

DIALOGUES: AGING

in gloucester harbor, almost exactly where we sat
in the house of another poet, one almost good as him
again on the porch and watched the work boats
gasoline to sea, and back, and called it beauty
I remember grey paint on the wood, old, peeling
a caved-in dock where townies, fucking, tossed
beer cans, underwear, discreetly, at night
the whole of it moving, slowly, to the oil and the water
it also making no sense that this was what was left
of gloucester, the boats still moving in and out
to the fish, the sea

       . . . .

not a chance, not one anymore
for me, you old devil
you, fool, to go there
but then again many times more the fool
she said, and I, seeing
it was said so plain, so right, believed her
you were too far out this time
the boat needed work
(it was not a skiff, nor was the brace for the oarlock missing) it was
just a boat needing work
of some sort
but of course it did not matter this time
that the seas were too rough for your judgment
the fog too clever for your sight

       . . . .

the pumpkins in your yard will rot
the saltbox, heated from ducts in the fireplace
will be sold
and the apples out back
will not remember you leaping from branches
their prize firmly in your hand
child of the sea
with no knowledge of it
knowledge only of apples
you should have played out back with apples
peopled your life with the things of good sense

the apples
and you, sez she, no one talks with such sentiment
about waves and beaten sand
you have forgot your origins, the changing of leaves
you have forgot your anger was faced with cider

. . . .

(it is all right, he said,
I heard it clearly, he was not mad
he said, going under
it is all right, I am going out
and taking the taste of it with me
you cannot take the taste of it from me
and I, it was amazing, it being so little
after his woolens and cadillacs
asking for nothing, just a taste
weeping because he was so free
laughing because he lied so well
but he blames me, even now
for spending so much time talking to water,
talking with women
it's all right, he said
have done with it
I'm dead
it's all right
I am not mad
have done with it
I am going out)

. . . .

thanksgiving, once, I saw them take it from the market
and even without seeing the killing, the dripping
the dressing
I could tell just from seeing it
it was not just a matter of what was eaten
and so I sat in the school auditorium
they proved to me even walt disney knew
snakes ate rats
they then said
put it in your music
go to college
go home
sleep on it
eat it
I did

. . . .

but it makes no sense
this sickness
tastes of autumn
it smells of wood burning
I am comfortable
it shows me leaves which fall to sidewalks
there is a cold air

(but here, don't you see, here
there is wood burning)

it is not the same

(here there are leaves turning)

but they are angry
they say, why are we doing that?

(but here—)

I just know that here
my sickness tastes of autumn
and it is impossible
it is a thing which makes no sense

M.L. Hester

HELTER-SKELTER

Sister went helter-skelter off
To Wyoming, that rectangular state,
With a man notorious for showing himself
To unsuspecting housewives at the zoo.
They saw another kind of animal there.
The cops were slow in finding him;
He was harmless, after all,
And one of their own kind.

Sis made mama cry; she said
The family was composed of strangers.
Dad had his feet in the past and
His head stuck in the future. No present.
Mama was too fond of wine, the sweet kind
You buy in supermarkets. I was destined
To work at a drill press and lose my thumbs.
Joey was still sane, but he was
Only seven. Give him time, she said.

The exhibitionist had hairy arms, a tattoo
On his chest, and drove a Buick.
He picked her up at noon, but kept
Himself hidden. That was gracious, but
Mama still fainted when the car
Was out of sight. I wonder if
There are mountains in Wyoming?

Susan Strong

THE MAN WHO DIED OF SHOCK

Brother John came to the cloister
seeking silence.
They showed him a room where he could write
but summer storms disturbed his peace.
At last his spirit left,
turning to the East
where silence opens slowly.
Brother John came to Bangkok,
seeking light.
They showed him a room
where he could pass the hot, damp night,
and gave him a fan to make electric breeze
but just when he bent to let it blow,
breathless in the darker bud of night,
Lightning came to make his silence bloom.

MERRY-GO-ROUND

The great golden stallions
Rise and fall to even measures
No horses of the sun, terrifying
They are securely pinned to earth
Turn within the turning of the earth.
Each horse descends for you to ride
Around the clock to where you stood before
Time past comes safely up to date and disappears
Each smiling horse, one foot politely raised,
Invites you to escape.

———————

Seen from above
Fog lies between the
Fir trees
Each one stands apart

Far from the others
In a field of brown needles.
Men clothed as princes
Emerge from the fog
Women dressed as gypsies
Soothsayers, with
Solemn faces.

———————

The door dissolves, powder is left
A light ash on the threshold
Let us place one foot-print
Here on this side, carefully.

Adriano Spatola

THE BOOMERANG

1

the weapon that turns against itself, the fish harpoons itself in the belly between waves of champagne

and: table well-set and: sparkling crystal: and I return (in a white jacket) to clean up the crumbs

all of us so well accomodated, nude, on the grass, to make a souvenir photograph

having decided on love in articulo mortis, a suicide: questions of modality settled on the telephone

having by now tried to discredit the debts we found mutually agreeable

shiny creases, fat: blue flash, the machinery melting

ripe fruit the elevator hanging and like the worm in the apple here I sit beating out spondees

2

I earn my pay staying two hours in the bath, writing gallant verse for old gentle ladies

but these starving bastards invade the piazzas, ruin the sidewalks, soak themselves with hydrant-water

I go get an aperitif—on the rocks, if possible—among those of my race, among my own people

but these starving bastards invade the piazzas, ruin the sidewalks, soak themselves with hydrant-water

with a casual gesture, there, I stop a cab: together we get away from them

but these starving bastards invade the piazzas, ruin the sidewalks, soak themselves with hydrant-water

and another who knew them all by now, even those in flannel, they beat him up: especially his comrade's wink

3

necropolis of the Dodge, of the wheelbarrows, of gutted pylons, of mobile gardens in which grass grows in the rain

necropolis: junk-tomb that the truck unloads on the riverbank, junk-heaps that the current erodes and carries out to sea

when the cement-mixer turns—sand, gravel and cement—in the piazza dug-up for a foundation two meters below street-level, on top of the live flesh of the city

and in the basements the family-crypt for typewriters, shelves piled with urns on which the dust drops from the new models

but under the shed, in the factory area, necropolis of bicycles—blind handlebars, saddles

with the bulldozer ravaging the lettuce patch, the man who wears an antenna crushes potted geraniums

parking-lot necropolis: to visit them late at sunset on the day of the dead, in the fog, November, opaque headlights, tombstone illegible

the dates of N and M are lit and go out, a variable arousing intensity

4

ah! that one digging in the road, the drill in the tooth

and nicotine settles right in the hole in the tooth

benzol secretions, methane sweat

and under the epidermis nestles the arabesque of branches that from deep within pump pus, rotating the scum of refined oil—the exhaust gas that colors the blood

christ! I want to really see them float, on the eel-shaped water of swimming pools: spit it up, you carrion: while breaks my

(tr. Paul Vangelisti)

Kit Duane

ANAIS

* One day I concentrated in the grass, and I managed to lift our house up several inches off the ground. This was as a result of my powers.

If you practice Yoga long enough, you come to a period of extra-ordinary powers. Sincere mystics do not indulge in a sideshow. They go on.

I didn't.

Our house is very old. The animals who ran out and hid in the garage must have been trapped under there for years.

Ours is not a regular garage. No cars can get in because there's no driveway and there's junk everywhere.

I called the zoo keeper. He looked. He'd never seen anything like either of them. He suspected rabies. He was sure they would bite. He suggested shooting them. I told him to go away. I brought out tins of chopped clams and cat food to the garage. The creatures stared at me. One was a beast. The other was something else again. She had brown eyes and sensitive ears. I could tell she liked music.

In the morning I waited until my children had gone to school before I got the extension cord out of the kitchen drawer and brought the record player over to the garage. My children would not have understood.

The furry, dark-eyed one crept out from inside Magic's old blue baby carriage. She was warm, a honey color, furry but sleek. I called her Anais. She danced to Segovia gracefully, on her fingers. She must have practiced under the house all these years.

I asked her how old she was, but she only looked at me with animal inscrutability. Her ears rippled while she listened to Segovia play "Granada." I believe her blood doesn't circulate but ebbs and flows.

I couldn't dance upon my fingers. Human fingers have cultivated sensitivity at the expense of strength.

When Colette came home from school, she asked me what I was doing with my fingers. I explained that I was strengthening them. Colette is nine. She looked at me severely.

Colette does not believe she is my child. She believes that she was born to a French count in the 17th century, and that she was whisked here by an evil time machine. She is sure she was meant for castle balls, a lavish wedding, early widowhood, and the saintly administration of vast estates. She looks upon our shapely house which I have painted lime green with red trim, and she says, "How did I get here?"

Children are always dissatisfied with their parents. When Colette was five I bought myself my own doll so I could play dolls with her. She explained that I should not play with my doll, but sit and watch her. When she did little things well, she wanted me to say, "That's wonderful, Colette."

So I did. I said, "My! You dressed your dolly up nicely."

That night I sat downstairs drinking tea and listening to Fargo. He was upstairs reading to the children from one of the books he has written on Balinese Raspberry Kings. Magic has always liked stories about kings. He believes he is destined to become king of a fertile volcanic island off the South Pole, inhabited by penguins and warmed by the Balinese current. Magic has not yet discovered the Balinese current.

When he came downstairs, I said to Fargo:

"Yesterday I lifted up the house several inches off its foundation."

"Fascinating," said Fargo. He went into the kitchen and poured us both a brandy. He sat down. "How did you do it?"

"Using my Yoga technique. I lay on my back in the grass, concentrating, and I said, 'rise house.'"

"I had a similar experience, Patch," said Fargo.

"Then perhaps Yoga isn't a prerequisite to miracles."

"Free will may be the prerequisite to miracles," observed Fargo, mellow and deeply philosophic.

"I admit that it's hard to believe in determinism if you can lift houses up at will."

We sipped our brandy, seriously.

"I saw Victor today," said Fargo, who looked penitent, but who nevertheless was chuckling. Mr. Victor was once our landlord, before we bought our secretive house.

"Why are you chuckling, Fargo?"

"He was walking down the street yesterday and he said, 'Good day, Fargo,' and I said, 'Howdy there you piece of shit.'"

"Oh how rude of you Fargo!"

"But he never returned our cleaning deposit, did he Patch?"

"Fargo, pick up the record player. We have to go to the garage."

Once again I found the extension cord and we moved our equipment down through the garage roof. It's fortunate that the roof of the garage has fallen in, because we don't have a key to the door.

Fargo and I sat on some old lampshades, shining pearly in the gloom, and put on our record of Segovia.

"Anais is very Spanish, Fargo."

Fargo loves Spanish women. One side of his nature would not object to cloistering me. Anais moved out from under a Rolls Royce engine left long ago by someone who had the key to the garage door.

Her ears were luminous and shone like opals. She came closer to Fargo and reaching out her sleek paw, touched his knee. She sniffed his crotch rather delicately, then climbed into his lap and licked his moustache.

"What an elegant, admirable creature," said Fargo. "What delicacy. What sublime subtlety. Perhaps I will dedicate to her my next Raspberry Book."

Fargo began to dance with Anais among the bundled newspapers and greasy pistons. She moved her ears like the tides of the sea. I watched them, tantalized. The moon shone through the roof. It was a lovely scene. Fargo dances gallantly. He has the dark eyes and the drooping moustache of a Zapata. He glistens in the gloom. Fargo loves Segovia with the passion of a revolutionary. He would ravage the countryside, leave women and children to die of hunger, rather then betray the soul of man.

"Segovia has no answer!" said Fargo once. "He is the answer."

The record became different by itself. It began to play itself on other scales, in other harmonies, without perfection, spinning quickly. Anais and Fargo began to dance faster and faster, spinning to the lost harmonies. They didn't realize I needed help because I couldn't cry out. The beast had put his hand over my mouth and squashed me into the pearly lamp shade. His violent nose was turning a hideous and horny trumpet. The beast's emerald eye glowed with bitter passion. The emerald eye looked into mine and paused. It watched for a token that I yearned for death in the dark, that I wished for his bloody angers, his gory nights. He sought in my eyes the voluptuous joy of the victim. But I made my eyes a mirror. A mirror of me as who I am. I am the Morning as Fargo is the Night. I turned my mirrors into his emerald eye.

The beast's nose began to soften. It became merely objectionable. I was surprised. Very surprised to have beaten the beast myself.

"Mother, what are you and Daddy doing out here!" Colette was peering through the roof. "Magic has wet his bed and he's crying."

"Why don't you help Magic into a new set of pajamas?"

"Because. That's YOUR job. I HATE the smell of peepee."

"All right."

"Daddy, you're not going to stay down there are you? This music is going to wake up the neighbors!"

Fargo followed me inside. He began to wash the dinner dishes while I went upstairs to change Magic's bed and his pajamas.

"It scares me when you go out at night without telling me," said Magic.

"But Magic, Daddy and I were only in the garage."

Colette leaned down from the top bunk. "But why were you in that horrible dirty garage in the middle of the night?"

"I have my own reasons, Colette."

"Oh I wish you weren't my mother," sobbed the French countess, sent here by an evil time machine.

Charles Klein

LATE LENNY BRUCE

not wanting to come out
   like a baby backstage
      in the birth canal
not wanting to be held up in the light
hear him screaming
morphine consuming his arm
                        a honey dew melon
the audience patience wearing thin :
   when's he coming out . . . more . . .
       injunctions
       arrests
       restraints
   the court orders you to appear
   on said date
   in the state of
   for the crime : obscenity
and he said—
          paranoia is the only healthy
          state of mind these days—
how well you took the doctor's prescription
but more
       going beyond mere talking
   marrying the stripper of your dreams
you were advanced like a shadow
getting on tonight late fumbling words
jokes missing
       pathetic
          someone said
         your performance
       showed just how sorry
     they were
     they saw you
            dying
              on
                stage

Susan Hoffman

she kept shoving me into the chair
beside the couch she was lying on
she made me listen
she made me say
aha
hmmm
yesss i see
she made me watch as she twirled a string
tighter and tighter around her finger
she made me watch as her finger grew
darker shades of purple
she made me listen to her stories
of past lovers and the hatred
she had for them all
she made me watch as her stiff purple finger
jerked and went limp
she made me laugh
at a dead finger in a living body

and then she made me hungry
she made me bite that dead finger
clean from her hand
she made me believe it was a gift
that would serve me well
she made me believe
i would be the best lover
she ever had

Judith Stone

BIRTH POEM FOR WESLEY

Like the dark Iowa earth
his grandfather brought to plow
there is a quietness in him
something fertile growing
in the fields of his face
long rows stretching out under his eyes.
His daughter is there in his face
a pheasant flying out from tall corn:
he would laugh with the sudden surprise.
She runs through his eyes
runs down through his large beard
runs down through his whole body
as if he had borne her
      he had been there
her first cry is raining down his face
and the fields of his grandfather's dreams
stretch out, bring forth his quiet face.

POEM FOR SARA

I wake up following sirens in the late summer night,
chasing them as they thin out into other neighborhoods.
And wondering from my dark upstairs room
seeing houses burning down
seeing long fabric hoses coiled like snakes.
And then when great blasts of water unwind
the full moon finally settles in through the window,
and the problem of the sirens is dissolved forever
in the particular light
coming down now across my daughter's sleep
and her grey cloudy cat curled against her belly.

POEM FOR TWO WOMEN IN A PHOTOGRAPH

The man in the photograph's face can be seen.
But the women's eyes hide in shadow
under the brims of large hats
and only the tip of the nose falls into the light;
And I wonder how the photographer could consent to this—
the heads drooping gracefully like the folds of cloth,
Acquiescent, as if the content of their lives
demanded they yield to the weight of a hat.
I run my fingers lightly over the old photo,
I see them step out of their carriage
and lift their veils
of shadow, I see them
drag their skirts down the dirt road
and leave them there
dead cloth.
Their eyes have gone out dancing
without their hats
weightless and without effort.

Aaron Poller

GHANDI REFUTES GRAVITY
for rodham elliott tulloss

peaches fly out of his mouth.
all the hair on his body
vanishes.
he cannot wear a tie.
it is said that he has hurled a stone
to the edge of the universe
where it appears in your dream
as an equation, something logical
you cannot refute in your life.

Sharon Williams

END OF DINOSAURS
(Pegasus)

They were not sleeping,
Leaning their long heads into the weeds
Their slow progress
Over the veldt stilled
They dipped their heads down,
Their scales settled,
Heavy bodies settled
      on their legs,
The great tree trunks
      hoisted and lunged
With them toward the banks
      of the slow river
Submerged, their eyelids
      drooped
Over lazy eyes.
Lucky, no curse had fallen
      on them,
They ate of the earth and all they desired
      fell to them
Sweet leaves, soft flesh, brown
      water on scaled shoulders
Only one thing, speed,
Only one thing, the air,
      eluded them
And they thought of it,
Long slow arc of primitive
      synapse
Slowly building thought
      like a river rapid
Pebble by pebble dams itself up
      in a pool
Till it spills over, the wall it has
      created, become
      a staircase
Spills over the bright spray
Of awareness, it breaks over
Flashing and sun-blinded
And throws its spray in long light crystals

And bright flat hands of whiteness
Obscuring the foliage
That crowds down to the stream
Obscuring their own legs and shoulders,
Their heavy presence;
It was slow in coming,
They had had all they wanted and never
      had to think,
Like a foolish brother
They wanted one more wish
      out of the cup,
And it came to them
The air, the air, Pegasus,
Taking off from the water,
Where their bodies fell
And were covered, where they shed their
      bodies and rose up, took off, Pegasus,
Where they dwindled as if in distance
And the air clothed them
Stroked its welcoming cloak of feathers
      out of their scales
And their great legs beaten
      in the forge of the air, flattened,
Full of physical knowledge, body
      without the mind,
The beloved objects
Stroked the air under
      the kindly favoring eye
Of their god.

PACIFIC THEORIES

What image can I tie this
      departure to?
As one who
      leaves the room   dies
As one who leaves a stage
    the tide comes in
      almost to the house pillars
In early morning the water
    is reflective, salt prisms
      break apart in flashes
They say, if you knew those lights

that break in the reef
shallows
You would know the sea.

Rain starts in the red hedges,
a face in the window
blurred by sheets of rain
I hide out   I travel
do not escape   do not arrive
I wanted to slow down
live like approaching tide
I wanted to go down
live by the sea in a shell
like a crab
tasting the tidepool
Alike and the rain water
splashed off the drooping leaves.

Carla Kandinsky

PARIS

At the booking in Palo Alto
Posing on a red velvet couch
And looking over the tops of easels
I pretend the trees
Seen through the studio windows
Are chestnut trees
And I am in Paris.
I think of you
Home at your desk, writing,
Wearing your olive jacket.
My mind wanders in and out
Of the radio music.
I consider buying some wine
On the way home.
Unconscious of time,
Wondering lazily if you
Stopped at the bakery.
The trees gold-green
Rush at the sky.
It is Paris and
I am very young.

CAMERA

"Stand still," she always said
Pointing the camera at us
Like a square weapon,
Daddy and me standing there.
Two victims, we were
Caught up in her command.
His arm around me
Protecting me from
He knew not what.
Stubby little man
Short fat girl
I mirror imaged him
In her camera eye.

I had his hair, his skin
His smile and sadness.
Her shadow there
In every snapshot
To one side
Or between us.

ARCO STATION

I feel like
An Arco station
Right on the edge
Of the desert.
You pull in
To refresh,
Nibble my neck
Like stale sandwiches
Drink me up
Like warm soda pop.
Refuel, rev it up
Roar out.
I turn out the light
Close up the station
All pumps are dry.

Who is that naked man in my kitchen?
He's pouring a glass of wine,
Coming back into the bedroom.
Oh well, he seems to know his way around.

Betsy Gladstone Huebner

THE PRISONER

Adroit and devilish
Full of slavish joy
Before the amulet of wisdom,
Art—we dove into
The whiplash chaos
Of our thought
And called each vision
If it held the cross
Of time and space
Reality.

We fish for God
With mirrors
Magnets, flesh.

His song askew, grotesque
Is ticklish, terrifying
Drenched in blood.

Christ is the prisoner
in your fist.
The broken dish.

ALASKA

The cold could kill
Slowly, if you were stuck
In a drift at forty below
And you curled up in the back
Seat, covered with newspapers;

Or swiftly at sea.
Before your lungs filled
With scathing brine your
Limbs would numb
And sleep would seem to come
As warm as love.

The sphagnum moss was so soft
Under the snow

Whole caterpillar tractors
Disappeared in it.
In the old days
Shanghied Philippinos
Walked out to the moss
To end their unpaid sleepless lives
As slimers in the cannery
By sinking slowly
And for good
Between the breasts
Of those green lowlands
I don't know how deep.

When the Stavros brothers came on their
Blue green salmon tender they said,
What are you doing here?

I was in love with the ocean, the danger,
The fish, the friend,
The urgency and mist,
And endless rain.

And the younger brother said he was "going
Down to Yakutat, it was so beautiful
There.   Desolate."

I loved what he said so much
I couldn't even
Understand it.

INHERITANCE

Your raving taught me how to hide
And hiding taught me how to find
The passage ways to air
So potent, tactile, clear,
No word is said, no thought disturbs
The lambent pool.

However, now my route through hiding
Is so deep engrained,
I fear I teach the ones I love
To rave.

MORNING

I do not eat breakfast
I do not comb my hair
I pick up the big white cat
And carry her out to the yard
Where I lie in the unmade bed
Of the rumpled clouds
Smelling of you.

Even the forest of hedges
Is blooming with
White flower balls
That grow in the fall
Like fur and are scented like people.

Even the concrete path
Rippled with leaves
Knows the softness of things and of grey
And embraces the clouds
And presses the feet of the cat
To its breast, to its lips
And sleeps
Dreaming of pearls.

BOAT POEM

Coot pumping
cross current
man gunning
docked trawler
gulls climbing
grebes diving
I glide in the nuance
reusing forgetful
elan and dispepsia
unwishful effulgent
genial glabrous
we lean on a dragon
and many will
lean on us.

Alicia Ostriker

WRINKLY LADY DANCER

Going to be an old wrinkly lady
Going to be one of them frail rag people
Going to have withered hands and be
Puzzled to tears crossing the street

Hobble cautiously onto buses
Like a withery fruit
And quite silently sitting in this lurching bus
The avenues coming by

Some other passengers gaze at me
Clutching my cane and my newspaper
Seemingly protectively, but I will really be thinking about
The afternoon I danced naked with you
The afternoon I danced naked with you
The afternoon! I danced! Naked with You!

ANNIE AND ME

Every truly beautiful girl needs a lump-type girl as a best friend
And the rules of their association, are, one, they confide everything to each
                                                                        other,
And, two, neither the beauty of the former, nor the lumphood of the latter,
Shall be acknowledged verbally by either
And my mommy said everyone was just jealous
Because of my I.Q.
Or—what?
Only she grew, a daisy, in my building—Annie—

In Annie's apartment I was shocked by the arrangements.
Five of eight snottynose kids in a bed, everywhere Mary & Jesus & saints
& knicknacks, behind the door hung a cat-o-nine-tails
I couldn't guess what it was until they told me
Nor could believe it used by Mister Hayward
That gentle alcoholic on relief—
Who walked me once to the subway and praised my posture—
Mister Hayward stood at that fifth floor window

And cried to his scolding wife and oldest daughters
"If you don't stop I'll jump!" They didn't stop, and he soared
Down to a spot in the hedged and wired garden.

My mommy, whose windows the Italian brothers broke
Again, because she hectored them not to play benchball *right* there
Said I could be popular
If I would remember to always be nice to people.
How could I? I hated people.
Annie got hips & bosoms early,
Many years ago we sat on the concrete stoop together in April,
I bet I sat like a slob, with my bloomers showing,
And I bet they were torn & dirty, and my socks had holes
I tried to tuck in my shoes
And that Annie in a see-thru blouse sat like a primrose.
"Do you know why I'm sorry my father died?" Silence.
"Who'll walk down the aisle with me now when I get married?"
O blush I ruby now for my gasp then.

My mommy read me books—I sat and drew—
The whole damned world played running away from me.
I would recall all this, old whelm, regurgitate.
Speak, memory, or I'll kick the shit out of you.

PORTRAIT OF A MAN

You wear glasses.
You wear blue flannel pajamas.
You are doing calculations on an envelope; and as you pause to think,
The lamp shines on your hands.
Here is your work, that you love
With a mad, faunlike, hidden mind.
Your profile, toward me, is not
Smooth as in boyhood.
Very well.
Some Ravel piano piece storms turbulently on the radio.
The heating system hums and rattles.
Like nested birds, our children sleep upstairs,
Not yet formed, but forming, becoming strangers.
Very well.
As for me, man, I'm watching your loneliness.

You sit in the dry light
And do not wish
To think of the winter approaching
With its wet black wings.

The light outlines
Serviceably the bumps
And indentations of your face and hands.
You scratch your blackhaired chest, under the pajamas.
Why this invisible dance ? This faithful striving for clarity ?
Ravel elaborates his terms of climax.
Having cogitated, you begin again to write.

PORTRAIT OF THE ARTIST
AS A PREGNANT WOMAN

Do I repeat myself
Very well then I repeat myself

I am a giant pear and eggplant, I make
Endless doodles of this superior shape

What a beautiful curve, I announce
The blooming belly naturally and exuberantly

Oblate, as loving is repeating, repeating
Is what I am loving, like a fat talking eggplant

Making a composition to smile about
And say, sing, draw, people, for you.

THE WOLVES

You were clearly pleased with yourselves
For having invented the wolves
I had to lug out from under
Your innocent beds, dear daughters,
Every morning, every damn morning
While that particular
Joke lasted, mommy crouching
To haul the heavy beasts out
By their bushy tails, hoist them and bear
On my back, out the door, down the stairs,
Out the front door, off the balcony
Five flights high—while in your nighties
Of small cotton, pink and pink,
You dreaded the fur and flank—
Each day, heaved them over the railing

And hurried back, shivering.
I did this for your sake;
You held your fright like a cup—
You dreamed them, and I had to break
Their necks, before you'd get up.

THE BRANDY OF PASSIONS

Self-loathing is the brandy
Of passions. I make it my favorite
Solitary drink, for its black twist,
For the deep way it burns the lips,
The throat and the heart.
God, it is very sweet, very sure, very pure.
And I like to dash it
In the faces of my enemies.
And I like to hurl
The glass to the stony floor.

REPORT FROM INNER SPACE:
SEAGODDESS, MUSE

"Yes, yes
That's what I always wanted,
To return to the body where I was born"

Yes, yes, that's all right for you, Allen,
That's all right for you, Robert C,
Because you were trained, as men,
To exist alienated from your hot flesh
Your pumping heart the nervous
Roadmap of your imaginations and
The whips of your instincts, but as for me,
Finally I'd like to get out.
You'd like to grow more feminine
But I've lived here my whole life.
Sure, I know it, I love it, I swim around here
All day every day, in fact that's my whole occupation,
Floating on my back, or diving, or whatnot,
And the fragrances are all infinitely precious,
The lapping of each wave infinitely sensuous,

The recurrent sucks & surges of the tides deliciously dangerous
And fascinating. If you want me you can find
Me here any old time, a-floppin around in this
Big old swimmin' hole — & that's just the trouble.
Let me out, man, I do need
To grow lungs & legs & give it a try —
I want some cold wheels
And a technological freeway
I want a gun like everybody else.

FIRST BETRAYAL

Remember back to then
O we were never behaving children
We stood and watched as all
The sky came down, like a white wall
Tumbling slowly
Ate apples in the snow
And stood and laughed. How could we know
We hung upon a crust, a dust, this place
A pebble pinned in space
                              O children, mind,
Infinity has driven angels blind
With whiteness; and they fell
Twisting, tearing their sky-speared eyes; and hell
Was limitless, the demons fall forever
Fall white, cease never
                              Foolish, we never guessed
Deceit, but always thought the snow was blessed,
As if the earth were solid and had roots,
We stood so steadfast in our shiny boots.

THE RAVEN OF DEATH

A grey November morning. We make love
Upon our marriage bed, strong, sweet.
Without a sound, the raven of death
Passes between us a black, serrated wing.
Across the long fields of Jersey and Pennsylvania
Corn stands in yellowed rows.
Oh life's companion, why must this be
Lovelier even than our filling each other?

THE SKY, ASLEEP, DREAMS A SNOWFALL

The lonely father soothingly releases
Us, like sick children, into the kingdom of rest.
A large conception has broken, falls everywhere.

It is so calm that the black car
Creaking through it becomes symphonic.
The driver inside feels perfect happiness.

PORTRAITE D'ARTISTE

When everybody's in bed
And you are away,
I'm alone, working on woodcuts,
Accompanied by a radio.
I print, revise, print,
I lay the ricepaper in rows on shelves.
I am trying, in this print,
To represent, simultaneously,
Two smoothed stones, such as one finds by the ocean;
Fruit—a pear for example;
And a torso, divided by a backbone and containing
A curled foetus. The colors
Are grays and pink oranges. I try also
To retain the wood grain.
The night is cold.
Meanwhile the hands on my watch
Go around and around.
Later I draw myself, with the baby inside me,
Standing in a long mirror,
Portraite d'artiste enceinte,
Ugly, proud, dignified,
Good bones after all,
Peaceful.

I think, "I was born lonely. I am best so."
And an artist at work can always
Be accompanied by death, which is happy.
But after all,
Most of my nights I spend with your hot body,
First fucking, then curled up together,
Then rolling around back to back and ass to ass,
Which, we have decided, or discovered, is best for sleeping

The whole night through—
I think my mother and father
Slept the same way, if
I remember correctly—
Even in sleep, not separated.

Rona Spalten

I AM HUNGRY TO EAT MY STOMACH

as if that embodied
  all the sap of the plant
  my body
flowers incessantly

OPHELIA

the mosaic i found
lied
it said i wasn't Ophelia
  and you weren't
hamlet
    Your small buildings cloister
    the sheriff said i was welcome to stay
              anytime
    said it explicitly, not to be mistaken
          or questioned
that would be fine with me
if i wasn't Ophelia
who screeches madly through the forests
at every touch of kindness

———————

the old man walks with his crooked back
hangs on to the lady's tits
with a train of buts about
the suitability of the clothes on
his crooked body his life
is a series of walking
to the men's room, washing his hands.

Ed Saucier

ROUGHNECK

oil feeds my family
fuck the oil spills, I'm working
7 on and 7 off
bring home that green
bustin my ass 12, sometimes 16 hours a day

throwing them air tongs onta that drill pipe
off again
on again
kicking the hell outta them six inch drill collars
I dare them to kick back
and you know what? I never even been close to a high school
but I sure do know what four hundred dollars a week
looks like. looks like I ain't gotta stand in all them lines
they got waiting
or watch my manners around the boss
or even give a goddamn about the economy
I know one thing: there's oil here
and I'm here

Quinton Duval

THE HEART SWAYS

Somewhere, inside you and me, our story is
dictated as sure as anything. A special section
under the belt, between the ears, wherever it is.
And the hard water of your crying gives while
taking away. In this puzzle, there is no clue.
No small diagram drawn on the backs of hands
and the insides of arms.
    It is maddening to see a little of your
inner room as the door swings shut.
That chair for me in there by the fire is what I want.
That newspaper with a good illegible headline.
Those slippers.
    You will never give me all this.
I can't get away without remembering my own
garden of eden. If you could see what's there
for you, you could talk to me about love, happiness
or some damned thing.
The angle of the heart is impossible.
It sways like a small lonely bird.
A hand passes over a red light and in that instant
the map of the soul illuminates. That is all we see.
And that band of night surrounding us.
Eyes with no stars.
Face with nothing left.
We follow that ancient route where nothing
has changed for a thousand years, and even
a blind man can tell us where we are.

Clive Matson

A RIGHTEOUS PALACE

The addict looks unobtrusive, flamboyant, tough
or cool, his face
is about the shade of a dirty sheet
and with its organic light shining inward,

his conscience inward too as he does
what he must to score and return
to a haven, continue the sensation
and the neutral quiescence of his soul.

The thought of every thought's the high:

the full warm rush inside,
                              total satisfaction,
strong feeling of well-being and
most buzzings and clashings are blotted or
can be with a little growling or manipulation,

— the room a chamber for his comfort,
the self become a righteous palace.

(And the mind can dream-stack ways of life
in a collage with a repeating theme,
smiling faces in the rip-off office,
teeth in the rip-off store

that support an easy country home
or penthouse luxury, vicious modes
and hypocrisies to attain a feeling
and glow similar to heroin's own.)

Sweet luxury! Lush opium,
warm yellow-pink haze shining through everything
so slowly, it's no pain
and easy motion as each thing turns slowly

on its side, each thing unfolds its arms
and reveals its being:
                              here a considered flower,
here a frozen flame-plume
and all textured mixtures in-between.

John Allen Cann

THREE POEMS DEALING WITH THIRST

Rain is a memory
his skin aches for
his tongue
slips between dances
into such
stillness
she bathes him
with the sweet white
of her hands

*

Your thighs
pitchers of cool water
I want to give them a slap
& make them splash

*

They feel the moon through the roof
the room wet with light
They lie in the tall space
full of dark tides
They slide toward
breaking the stillness
each moment they melt away
Outside the window an owl whoos by the creek
They begin to drink
to drown into each other

Patricia Dienstfrey

BLOOD AND THE ILIAD:
THE PAINTINGS OF FRIDA KAHLO

It is not that her brains were dashed in battle
And ran to the ground

> Or that her eyes all bloody dropped in the dust
> Or that she cried out, god-like, a loud war cry

> No, we see this is not so from her paintings

But that her body was impaled on a metal bar
In an accident that crushed her spine

That her life was a life of battles with physical pain

> For which she decorated herself with jewels and lace
> And braided her hair with ribbons

That she painted in a wheelchair
Or lying in bed under a mirror

That she painted herself

> In a surgical landscape
> Chin set on a broken Ionic column

> Nails like the nails from Christ's cross
> In her breasts
> And scowling face

That her nurse was a Mexican goddess

> Whose milk fell in a white forest
> Where leaves grew clean
> And pallet-shaped

That she lived in Detroit with her husband Diego Rivera

> In the Henry Ford Hospital after a miscarriage
> She hemorrhaged

> She lay like a newborn
> In a nest of blood

> Blood, how gorgeously she painted it

> It splashed into a bucket by her bed
> From a clay heart
> From cords she snipped

Her thoughts grew on six blood stems

    A breast-penis
    A Diego-like child
    A cut flower from the white forest
    A womb, unravelled
    An iron clamp
    A stainless pelvis

When Diego left
She cropped her hair

    And it fell on a blood-red floor
    Under the lyrics : *Mira que si te quire, fué por el pelo*

She used red every morning

    As gems
    As plum on her lips
    As fuschias in a headdress of pleats and braids

And when it was finished
When black lovely night rolled down

No cry rose to assault the lamp of day

    But ghosts came back as they do
    To blood-stained ground and drank from her hands
    Her white fingers

    Where she had scraped away the paint

WHEN ZEUS THE THINKER
BEGINS TO SNOW

Almost everyone in this dream is lying down
One man, a scholar, is lying in a field

One woman is grinding roses and salt
in a mortar

But the king stands in a quiet pool
It must be a compass

When he speaks his subjects who float
change direction

    When he drives swords into women's feet
    they appear on their heads as crowns of flowers

An old woman keeps souls in order
in a room of shelves

                        white as sheets

When I look down

               She is a mountain

When the souls hear voices

          They open their mouths and fall as snow

                        I am the one who is dying

Everyone in the valley has brought their faces close
to mine — the orphans, the scholars, the murderer-king

Though I cried for the women

           He lay behind me and pulled me in

                   whispering

When Zeus the thinker begins to snow
I think of the king

        So dark and long
        Above my head and below my feet

        And of pleasures I have known

                 on a string of shame

That the name he whispered is written

             in a cupboard of bone

That the woman leaning over the mortar was gold
A twin of the king's except

        Her colors were under her skin, burning

She must have given *me* the drink

I remember standing in the kitchen
The first labor pains came from a pool
below my spine

        They tasted of sugar

PEARS, SNOW, MOONLIGHT

Someone said the old man
came out in winter with no clothes on,
and from a ladder
that looked silver in moonlight
picked pears from the tree—

Which is why my friend Cay and I
looked in his window.
An old woman in a dress
with no collar or cuffs
was giving him a bath from a porcelain set tub.
With his hair wet his head
looked like a skull behind glass
in the Boston Museum.

We risked broad daylight.
The house was on a corner,
clear to the streets.
Not one stick, stone or leaf
hid us, except the tree,
which was dead.

But it was worth it to see.
Her hair rolled into the dark room,
thin as smoke.
Her apron, tied in a firm knot
and bow, stared out
behind her back.

TOMATOES IN NOVEMBER

Tonight when I came up the back porch stairs,
and saw redwood benches
slick from rain, and tomatoes
in a line in the window to ripen in November
because I planted them late in May,
I remembered a lunch of tomatoes
my mother made.
She fried bacon first,
then tomatoes
in the bacon fat
and a batter she tried to make crisp,

but which stuck half raw to the tomatoes.
The rest came up in black chips in fried eggs—
A meal we ate an hour
after my friends had finished their lunches.

I could hear them play in the back lot
while I sat at the table enraged,
because I didn't like the taste
of cooked tomatoes,
and my mother, flushed,
enjoying her meal,
talked past me to my father,
who didn't often come home for lunch—
which was I can see now,
the occasion.
Yet for some reason I stayed.

When I did leave,
on the back porch the glare
and dust and first
bite of fall air
in the heat
was a sharp, quick pang.

SECOND TO LAST AUTUMN

she stands in a door
in thick yellow light,
back pressed to a black world
tinkling with tiny lights . . .

she in a windbreaker and riding boots,
smelling leaves and leather,
light-headed with New Hampshire autumn cold
and dreams

       of rides of rescue on horseback
      she on a rearing
         red
            black
               white
                    horse
           flare-nostriled

pounding,
the long walk home
from the barn . . .

and standing,
watches the room grow unfamiliar,
confused by a basket of apples,
too red for the shrinking kitchen,
her mother at the sink cutting squash,
grows shorter, grayer as she turns.

"Patsy, where have you been?"

carwheels bite the driveway gravel,
her father back from seeing patients;
his step firm behind her,
she goes in.

it is
the second to last autumn
she will fit.

NAT

Nat, fourteen,
calls his cat at midnight —
Ki — tty —
whistles like a flute.
Some mornings
he doesn't go to school
walks out in his bathrobe
the cat in his arms.
They sit in the sun;
Or he borrows
his father's tools
to work in his mother's garden
prune the trees
and mow the lawn.
Afternoons, he sweeps the walks,
waters his flowers
fuschias, impatiens, petunias
and fights with the girl upstairs
his shouts so harsh
I think they must hurt his throat.
She kicks his flowers.

And when my children
pick his lemons
and tramp the grass
he shrieks and twists their arms
and they throw dirt clods.
Evenings his brother comes
leans on his leaky Honda;
Father and brother talk.
Nat is silent.
But when he calls his cat at midnight
his voice is clear,
goes easily over the garden
as if the world were empty.

THIN PATCHES

Some time out on thin crystal
out where space is high domed, oval,
days on the high edge of shatter,
each bird a wing-pumped spark;
Out nights when small silences sing,
and the sound of trains rides over
the height of the dark oval,
the inexplicable houses,
the hot-blooded bodies
tucked in small white squares . . .

In December we went out skating,
hot cheeked, glided the lakes from end to end,
around dark-shrubbed islands,
made whips and figure eights,
bodies tuned to the low sure skim
of blade on solid ice;
And all the days we skimmed,
we carried in the narrows of our brains
cracks, and sudden plunges.

Paul Bendix

FERN DEATH IN THE AFTERNOON

"I regret to inform you that our fern has died." Camille was holding the drooping, withered little plant in her slender hand, and tiny clots of Super Soil went tumbling down her forearm as she spoke. She stood noble and erect, the small of her back arched in a bony crescendo, while she thrust the potless, barerooted green thing in my face.

"I am sorry," I said, turning away.

"Sorrow," she replied, with a nimble little turn of her foot, "is cheap. Why don't you water things? You water yourself—why don't you water a green, dependent plant? Suppose you had to fry in the hot sun without a drop of water?" Camille strode to the wastebasket and brushed her fern into its metal depths, rubbing the dirt from her hands as she spoke. "I hardly need to remind you that neglect of living things is a global problem. It exists within ecosystems, between people on park benches, between people on Park Avenue. We entrusted this fern to you, because we believed you were ready for it. You have failed, and there is very little I can do. I will have to speak to Max."

"Camille," I implored, pulling her toward me, "please don't tell Max. Come on, be a Girl Scout. Be decent, and, honestly, I won't forget it."

She touched my cheek and gazed with hard, puzzled eyes. "Yes, it is a pity. Max will not be pleased that our union has yielded nothing more than a dead fern. Honestly, I don't know what he will say. You must expect him to exact penance, though, my darling. Remember: Max is God.

Max was God, and not in any phoney, symbolic sense of the word. Max was God in the deific, ultimate, omnipotent sense. I mean, he was God, damnit. In the beginning there was the word, and the word was Max. Max said, "Let there be light," and there was. Max caused the waters to part. Max foresaw the invention of the wheel, the evolution of antlers, the demise of polystyrene and a host of other things. Max was the host of other things. Max is part of you and me, and we are Max, and he thinks about us every day, wherever we are on that grand arcing highway that begins and ends with dust.

I discovered Max one day in Palm Springs. I was tryng to dial Joanie from a pay phone at the airport, when a lush, lovely sound filled and transported me. I almost bit into the receiver from the sheer joy of it, and my arms rose along the glass walls of the booth, seeking in the metal joints and folds, the fluid, sprightly nectar of sound that dripped and flooded my mind. I was standing on one foot now, almost bent over from the excruciating vibrance of the dense and wafting tones that came near and far, falling full upon my head, casting me gently to and fro.

Finally Max spoke. His voice seemed to come from the receiver, but I instinctively knew better. "Compose yourself," he said. "Someone saw you acting strangely in the phone booth and has summoned an airport guard. This guard is a gruff and pleasant man, originally from Chicago. A reference to that city should get you off the hook."

I told the guard that I was talking to a funny friend in the Windy City, a real card, who was killing me with his jokes. The guard almost smiled, and he walked away.

"Now," said Max, "this was bound to happen sooner or later. You know who I am, of course, and I won't bore you with long-winded explanations about communications satellites and so on. It should suffice to say that I am at your service. You are, doubtless, aware of the three-wish motif that runs like a river through the world's cultures. Well, my friend, you have just that: three. I suggest that you consider for a moment the mistakes of your predecessors, before you plunge into anything rash. Take your time."

The phone booth was filling with a golden fog. Max's voice had an awesome, caressing ring to it, and I stood, dizzy and ecstatic at his very breath echoing through the foggy chamber. While I considered his offer, he said: "You may call me Max."

My voice rang shrill. "Max, I can't believe it. How will I pay for this call . . .?"

"Don't worry," he said. "It's on the house."

Pinpoint shafts of blue light burst from the tiny holes in the earpiece, and no matter where I held it, I could hear Max, loud and clear. I realized, watching the swirls and eddies of the particulate golden vapor, that it drew from me the power to doubt and question. It sucked incredulous little nothings from the side of my head, just below the temples, and in their place, in the space where despair, distrust and fear of the moment fought valiantly to enter and possess my cortex, Max infused more of his Elysian mist. It entered my bloodstream (I could feel it) and coursed dizzyingly to my brain. The laser threads of blue intensified from the receiver, which I let dangle. "Three wishes," Max intoned. "I call your attention to the Brothers Grimm and remind you to be cautious."

While Max spoke, I watched a doubt (the suspicion that someone had put drugs in my coffee) emerge, a curling, matted web of lines, and disappear in the shimmering mist. "Max," I said finally, "can I phone you back? I just can't make up my mind about the three wishes. Look, I'll give you my number at home, if you want."

Max's laugh was positively operatic, and when it subsided he said only, "No, my friend. This encounter is known on your earth as a 'mistake' and you will not pass this way again—at least not by phone. It's now or never."

"Tell you what," I said to Max. "Just forget the whole thing. Take back your wishes and go on hurling those slings and arrows—just go a little easier, OK?"

"Wheee," someone squealed. I noticed that a flock of elfin persons, tiny seraphim of some sort, sat cross-legged on the phone box, clasping their sylph fingers and shrieking with delight. While I stood, transfixed and warmed by their porcelain features, I watched another doubt (the belief that they were transistorized) slip into the precious ether.

"Congratulations," said Max. "You have solved the riddle of the universe. You and a few others. We will be in touch. Better tell them the phone is broken." These last words made precious little sense to me, and they hung in the air, which I noticed was indeed now merely air. I also noticed that the airport guard was again outside the phone booth and that he had a policeman with him. I picked up the receiver, dropped it gently back in its chromium home, and strode nonchalantly into the milling lobby. "Phone's shot," I said to the two cops. I pretended to heed the final call of a flight to Phoenix, looking earnestly for the right gate.

Camille gained swift access to my apartment house, merely flashing a health inspector's badge in the doorman's face and jumping in the elevator. Later I asked why she had resorted to this elaborate ruse, why Max had not supplied her with, say, a vial of golden dust. She looked tired, saying only, "You're such a romantic." She always wore the same outfit when she came to see me—cashmere sweater (green), tweed skirt and jacket—and her hair, even after hours of lovemaking, hung pert and pretty about her angular, knowing eyes. And the sequence—after the first momentous day—was always the same: to bed, lecture, to bed again, more lecture, and then discussion. The obvious disdain and even displeasure with which she regarded our lovemaking occurs to me only in retrospect. I recall the first time she threw off her clothes and lay sideways, like an ivory piano, cold and composed, on my bed. I sat down beside her, but her steely repose and obvious ennui did not arouse me. I felt very small and everything about me shrank and retreated. I ran my eyes and then my hand along her lithe and unresponsive length. "You admit of no entry," I said sadly. "You must come close," she said, and as I did so, I noticed that the skin about her breasts exuded wisps and fine clouds of golden vapor. I pressed nearer to the source and felt stupefying fear and reluctance flushed free at my temples, drawn by the mists, and beneath her blank and absent stare, I warmed, hungered and sought knowledge—just like in the Bible.

She insisted on rapt attention during her lectures, and I often had to drink coffee to keep awake. She drew the sheet over me and sat in a chair, impatient to impart as much as her limited time allowed. While she spoke, if my eyes wandered, or if a fatuous smile betrayed some lighthearted thought, she would tower and rage, saying always, "Max has kept his bargain—you must keep yours." It seemed that over the eons a handful of people and others had stumbled on old Max, and an even smaller minority had spurned the three-wishes ploy, thereby earning what Camille said she was delivering: the Celestial Truth. She said that the only other human recipient of Max's graces was at that time living in Valparaiso, Chile, a woman who had picked up Max on her short-wave in 1953, and casting aside the wishes, now received weekly visits from Camille, just as I did. Camille refused to say what she did with her off hours, and fairly bristled when I asked what sensual raptures she dispensed to the woman in Valparaiso. These were candid questions, asked politely during the discussion period, and it endlessly infuriated her to see her genius wasted on such a lout as I. Did I realize, she demanded to know, how many men could boast of making love to their own animas, unimpeded, in a pure celestial haze? None, came the answer, as she pounded her fist against her hand. Did I appreciate that a messenger from the godhead sat opposite myself, that her lectures on illusion would ultimately cause my very walls to crack and buckle, my apartment to collapse (she would warn me)? Did I realize that men had flayed and cauterized themselves just to have a brief chat, say, in the final fifteen seconds of their mortal lives, with her—and not been granted even that? I looked about the room, during these reprimands, always wondering what this icy stainless woman had done to make me so happy.

In the discussion periods my mind was often a blank, and I groped for questions. Was he always called Max, I once asked? How did I get him on Joanie's number? Who put Max in the driver's seat? Why did he feel obliged to delight my body and instruct my mind? She never answered these questions, for there was always one question, the question, which I was supposed to draw from her lecture and to pose, compelled and awestruck, to her, my instructress . . . . "Heaven must be full of that golden gas," I remarked one day, patting my stomach and giving Camille a knowing little wink. Our discussion always ended at 5 p.m., and Camille was out of the door faster than the devil.

My daily life became infused with thoughts of Camille beside me on Saturdays, golden fog running in delicate banks down my pillow. The days in between began to fade and recede from my mind. They took on the quality of a certain conversation I had once heard between two colleagues in the morning elevator. They were talking about electric garage doors. The flavor, the garage-door blankness of that conversation set the tone of my days away from Camille. At work I felt that my desk would all but slip its Cosco moorings and float ceiling-ward like some fluorescence-seeking missile. At times I would grip the rubber edges of my desk and lean forward, like a passenger at the rail of a ship, and the carpeted sea, the very garage-doorness of the walls came surging at right angles, and I longed for a little hit, just a whiff, of that mist—to sort of put things right.

"I really want you to promise me that you'll see Dr. Erline this time. Really make an appointment and see him. And, for Christ's sake, George, tell him everything. Tell him you're losing interest in work—and in me. Tell him about those Saturdays you spend barricaded in your flat, doing God knows what. Tell him, because if you don't . . . ." Joanie pushed her fist against her mouth and began to sob in a way that made me want to take the candle at our table and burn a sizeable hole in my cheek. I hunched low over my coffee and took her hand. She was biting her knuckles and I hoped the waiter wasn't looking.

"Look, Joanie," I said, "have you ever noticed how good I feel on Sundays? I mean, you come over and we go out or we stay in, and you talk and I listen, and the day goes, just effortlessly, like a dream. Don't you think so? Is that bad? It's not for me. I love it."

"George . . . ." She stirred her coffee and her eyes hung, spilling sadness on the crisp tablecloth. She set the spoon down, sighing, and held her cup in both hands, eager for a little warmth. "I don't believe you're seeing another woman . . . . I don't think you're taking drugs. I want you to see Dr. Erline. Please, for me."

"I'll tell you the truth, Joanie. I'm a gold dust junkie."

"Very funny, George."

"Joanie, what if I'd found a way—a way to know more, a way to get more . . . ." There was no describing it—Max had seen to that, somehow—and Joanie must have noted the dim, idiotic gaze that came over my face, for she hastily unclasped her purse and thrust Dr. Erline's card across the table.

"Please, George, for me."

5 October
Dear Max,

I am writing you this, knowing that you are reading it before I even think of what to say. So I will not mail this, much less tape it to the phone booth in Palm Springs, as I had originally intended. Here's the thing, Max: No more Camille. No more. I passed up the three wishes, so OK, now I pass up wonderwoman and her joy dust. Kindly send her away, for she is ruining my life, six days a week. You have made your point, just like in some fable I can't recall now: Joy is beyond us mortals. I concede the issue and have learned the lesson. She has to go. Also, I am very sorry about the fern. Camille had devoted two lectures to it, and I was very pleased to have a token of celestial something to remember her by for the rest of the week. At night, when I turned off the light, I loved to look at the shimmering green glow that danced among its fronds. I guess Camille made her point about life and energy and so on, but I really don't care very much. I think that's why I didn't water it. Thanks for trying to teach me, but now I want out.

All the best to you,
George

On the following Saturday Camille didn't even bother to knock. She slipped a passkey in the lock and quietly stepped inside the door. She stood, her long arms clasped behind her, her head tilted sadly to one side, that damnable what-fools-these-mortals-be expression written all over her face. "Come," she said, "we have a long way to go." She walked, silently, absently, to the coffee table and deftly slid her purse to the glass top. Inside she retrieved an apparent pack of Rol-Aids and unwrapped them; from paper to foil to tablets, standing like a musing stork. "Here," she said, "this was Max's idea, not mine," and with a tender and swift thrust of her hands, she pressed the white tablets against my eyes.

The room began to shower and to snow, drifting white, like a winter paperweight, and the glowing flecks cascaded down the walls and sped against the door. They slid in eddies across the floor and under furniture, banking in corners and winding delicate tendrils of flake and essence around Camille's slender legs. She stood, encased in a shroud of her own golden vapors, and her eyes opened in a sad and telling way. She extended her hand, and as I rose to join her, the white, spectral flakes began to rush and enter the forms of the room. I stared at my armchair, now a dizzying dance of chair particles, clutched, caught in chairness, woodness, leatherness, in awesome trammelled frenzy. I looked at Camille, who shrugged, as though to say, "Yes, this is how it is." She led me out and down and through the alley where my car entered and left the garage. She led me across town and over the river. We climbed towers and descended canyons, or perhaps, only crossed bridges and turnpikes, everything whizzing in zig-zags and spinning powdery bits. When we came to the forest, she eyed the surroundings with distraction and annoyance. She strode about in a clearing, stepping among brush and branches, and calling at last to me: "Here. You're supposed to do it here." Suddenly everything stopped rushing and congealed. Leaves fell, horns honked, the breeze blew, and before me, in a rather dull neck of the woods, Camille stood, vaporless and beckoning.

"Do what?" I asked.

"Root," she said, and as I stepped forward, my feet shot tubes into the earth, my arms sprouted fronds and I noticed, after a few moments, that I bent and swayed to the rushing wind. I don't to this day know what Max has in mind, but I think a lot and seldom sleep. There are worse fates, and I'm not allergic to the spores.

Mario Donatelli

EN CETTE MOMENT LA/VERLAINE'S VERSION

Finally
advertising has stolen
more from your poems than the critics, Rimbaud.

Because visions passed like water among friends
are collected in buckets for gain in the morning—

And they say it is because of your silence
that the corners of the market are so square
they say you were a child hewing stone
and your hands happened to fit the axe

they say you carried blades in your sneakers

But I have seen your weapons
weeping like mice
in the golden fields of your head
I have met you in the darkness
and not knowing of your conquests
and the interpretations to follow
only feeling the river of your hair
tangling my own

would not make love to you

was that the night you stopped writing poetry?

They are making money off your soul
and we are looking through windows
that refuse to close

I no longer ask you for poems
only the sound of your voice

Milo Miles

LOVING YOU AGAIN

The line of naked men
winds down the beach,
muscles slack and grey,
salt drops in the evening sun.
Let me torture them. In my bedroom
sits the barrel of eyes,
the cabinet of tongues,
my silver pruning shears . . .

The girls drive to places
with vulgar names—Albuquerque, Minot.
A dry haze rings
the town, only the sun escapes.
Deep in the mirror, a white chip
rising, say the Orca, a lotus turning
on dark blood, try loving you
again

I take down the pewter mugs
finish the warm beer. Windup music
on the radio. Jet planes lifting
sear the fog—
your shift is zipped, nose
on straight, chainbreaker,
shitslinger,
finder of seashells & men.

Michael Covino

COMPOSITION AND DECOMPOSITION

For D.S.

At the lake shore when I was little
I changed into my swimsuit
in the cinder block dressing room
with the puddles on the floor.
Then outside at the canteen
when Kathy's ice cream scoop tumbled off the cone
I gingerly picked it up,
brushed away an ant and a twig
and mounted it back on,
with a tap,
to secure it.
We walked down to the water and she listened enthralled
as I spilled over with story after story —
the time me and my friend Allen spent the recess dipping
  Phillip's head in the toilet,
and the other time — at Gary's request — when we wrote the perma-
  nent absence note explaining he wouldn't be able to attend school
  any longer because he'd drowned while looking in the sewer for
  the basketball.
She was enchanted and I was enchanted, and at sunset
holding hands still a bit sticky with ice cream
we watched the lake fade from blue to black.

After the high school dance
we pulled into the service station,
saw people walking around in the white glare of the fluorescent
  floodlights,
"Characters with no future," I thought and climbed out —
The pop tune on the airwaves cried
Who will be your lover tonight?
I twanged the car antennae,
Carol banged on the windshield *Stop that!*
pretended I was in another land,
was in another land.
Then Terry double-parked outside the liquor store
while I ran in for a six-pack,
and from the top of the hill,
the night air cool against my face,
I looked out at the distant fiery night factories

and farther back, beyond the highways that ringed the city,
the twinkling housing projects massed against the black horizon,
then laughed suddenly when I remembered I lived there.
"What's so funny?" she said.
"Once upon a time," I began unevenly,
"after shaving, I sat still for an entire day,
my fingers lightly touching my chin,
anticipating the return of stubble."
But for that I received an uneasy look.

As the plane climbed through the quiet night
I watched the last light fade off the starboard wing.
And when the shimmering lights of a foreign city
wheeled beneath the wing
it occurred to me
there was no one to call.
I was lost in these thoughts,
hauling the suitcase around the terminal,
then while riding the escalator down
my elbow bumped a girl's doll
off the moving handrail.
I bent to get it
and put my suitcase on her mother's foot,
stumbled over my words in my rush to apologize
but she laughed easily.
Then in the cafe
everytime I tried to tell her about myself
the words were drowned in the crackle of a departure announcement.
Yet even the airport terminal with its searchlights crisscrossing the
    dark skies seemed to shine with the promise of a new day!
We rode the expressways
over the far-flung suburbs,
flat, glimmering,
with the blue airfields behind
and the city looming ahead, its world-familiar silhouette.

—There was no warning.
My body suddenly ached with a fear
so absolutely present it was impossible to name
but this land's end feeling then diminished
as we left the expressway and moved through the quiet
    residential streets,
and in the cold morning
amongst the new sounds
when the child slipped into the bedroom
—a foreign paper landing with a slap on a distant doorstep—

—the clanging of the milk bottles down a cobblestoned street—
on such a morning
with the child bouncing up and down on the bed,
her wide eyes bright with expectancy,
the sudden desire to tell her a story—
: a minute passed . . .
not knowing what to tell.
And in the light of a new day turned suddenly old,
amidst the discord of the new old clatter,
I faltered—

UNFREE ASSOCIATIONS

for Reggie Jackson and Andreas Baader,
October 18, 1977

In the stadium one bright, fall morning
when Willie Mays stepped to the plate
everyone rose from their seats as one
—there was a poetry in the way he held the bat—
and with the Giants and Yankees tied for the series
and a tie score in the top of the ninth
the whole world seemed to hang in the balance . . .

Stretching around the curvature of the outfield wall
the advertising posters flashed in the sunshine
while in center field Mickey Mantle
fanned himself with his cap.
It was very quiet in the stadium
there was a three-and-two count
and when Whitey Ford went into his wind-up
I squeezed my father's hand.
Crack !—Mantle drifted back,
then broke into a run
but when he dove for the ball
he slipped, slamming up against the wall :
above him, a poster— *Capri, the Sexy European*
A woman sat on the hood of the car
with such aplomb I found it unnerving,
and even as Mantle leaped up to chase the ball
which had ricocheted off the wall
I couldn't tear my eyes from the poster . . .

Years later
while driving my Capri to work at dawn
a billboard rose before me,
a two-hundred pound football star,
in helmet and shoulder pads,
there was poetry in the way he held the toothpaste,
and when I looked out at the pine trees that landscaped the freeway,
their tops tossing in the early morning wind,
I was overcome by a sudden surge of emotion
and wanted to break open the cellophane on a new pack of anything,
then roll down my window and take a deep breath—

In my capacity as copywriter it was my duty
to try and rescue the secret but logical connections
between objects and the feelings they evoked,
to try to make life itself
more and more evocative . . . .

But in the years that followed
more and more
wherever I went
something would remind me of something else—
And though it only seemed natural to glance at the long glass
rows of bottles in a liquor store window, and think of pine
trees mounting a snowy hillside—
Or to hear someone in the next room smoothing out a sheet of Alcoa
aluminum foil, and suddenly feel transported to a long white Car-
ribbean beach with surf crashing all along it—
Still
after each storm
I would find myself searching the changing skies for the comforting
yellow arches of McDonald's—
And whenever I passed a Woolworth's,
whenever I would see the bubble gum machine out front
—the round glass case filled with colorful balls—
I would suddenly long for the din of a big city playground,
the downcourt dribbling of basketballs,
the jangling of backboards—
then the last cries at dusk.

In this way
as the years went by
the time and space of my world grew strange
until the whole world seemed to ache
and everytime the sun went down
it seemed to pull part of the horizon down with it.

And once when I dropped a tube of haircream on the bathroom tiles and it bounced, I thought — companionship.
When I left the carton of ice cream sitting on the table and returned later to find it hadn't melted — integrity.
My supermarket purchases in the big crisp bag — an autumn lane, a pumpkin stand.
The plastic yellow shower curtain in all its shimmering radiance — school children hurrying home in the rain.
Yes, and the new red blender on the formica counter — my father taking me after dinner to the snowy lot behind the housing project to help pick out a Christmas tree.
Then again, on a winter night through a frosted window the blue glow of a tv screen — the fear is settling into the streets and the world is coming home.

FALSE PHRASES

When the world is reduced to a cold, bright morning, — a beach for two faithful children, — a potato in all its earthy holiness, — a single note of song, — we shall have vanished.

. . .

My father's childhood home, white clapboard house, small town New England, — the potatoes pushing up in the back garden, — the mailman whistling down the leafy street, — and look ! — "That diesel pulling the line of linked flatcars. . . .*Maine!*. . . .*Pacific!*. . . .See how the engineer waves to me !"
Late October, the gypsy girl and I, — we walked barefoot down a Nova Scotian beach at dusk, — she dipped her hand into a tidal pool and withdrew a perfect seashell, — we cooked periwinkles over an open fire that night, — and slept beneath the stars, —

. . .

And even if it should be true, —
still, —
on a cold, clear morning
the last coal goes out
and the words begin to draw back from the observation.
altering forever the nature of the observed.

. . .

QUESTIONS:
What was the tune the mailman whistled? No tune, nothing at all,
he was shy and had a harelip.
But then what about the leafy street, what about— ? And up and
down the leafy street, massacres and mergers are being hatched.

But did the seashell not sound like the ocean? Did the— ?
No, for a jet was climbing in the dusk,—
for a clumsy sandcrab lowered itself from the shell into your ear,—
for two faithful children—O come on now!—are never faithful,—
and anyway you were alone,—

and anyway you never got that far north,—
and anyway—well—you get the picture.

but the words? the phrases? the— ?
Shoddy salesmen working on commission,—you should never have
said, "Come in," but *"Keep moving,"*
But the dreams! the dreams!
And even the nature of our dreams has changed.

But then what about the potatoes pushing up in the earth?
What about the white clapboard house?
For far behind the auto body shop the distant fields lie fallow,—
And on the railroad siding beneath the shade trees the potatoes are
rotting (at an undisclosed price) in heaps on the unattended flat-
cars,—
And the white clapboard house is exploding like a pile of debris
into a thousand cities twinkling on the edge of this changing night.

IT'S BEEN SO LONG (LANDSCAPE)

> "Hello . . . ? Is anybody home?"
> *The Texas Chainsaw Massacre*

It's been so long.   You're driving through the countryside, the
morning air is cold and bright.   But out across the low-lying
fields, the ground fog clings to the legs of the billboard.

As the day wears on, you whisper, "Like in a dream, everything's
just like it used to be."   But already one's thoughts are turning
away.

In the rearview mirror: someone in a long, dark coat is walking
along the edge of the road.   And that old, familiar feeling of
traveling through a strange country is taking hold.

The car glides through the park at dusk, and the woods creak all around.   If there's anyone in there, they remain hidden.

Just as the car reaches the blinking red traffic light, the rain starts gently falling.

And though the cool, wet air still feels pleasant enough, the maples have already begun to go red.

: and the storm clouds break apart in great, slow motions—

: the last light seems strangely flattened and compressed—

: and through the drizzle, across the valley, a car climbs the remote slope and disappears over the far ridge.

THE DIRECTOR OF DEATH

The doctor had finished talking. The man, shaking his head in disbelief—he was dying of cancer—rose from the large black leather chair and left in stunned silence. At the door he glanced back at the doctor whose smile, meant to be comforting, seemed only enigmatic and cruel.

It was early twilight. The walk home was long and the man tried to forget himself in the sights along the street: the hams hanging in the butcher's window; the ghost masks and skeleton costumes—it was late October—in the novelty shop. And when he passed a candy store with the evening edition already posted, he was suddenly so unnerved by the headlines with their hideous grammar that he wrenched up his coat collar, then speeded up his pace. Though he was a retired teacher, no one had ever asked him for his own educated but superfluous opinion.

Just then a line of street lamps came on together; he looked at his watch and saw it was already six. And where were the church bells? Why weren't they tolling! Storm clouds were gathering over the low mountains to the north where it already looked like nightfall. From far away came the screech of a car; he tensed, waiting for the smash of glass and metal, which never came.

"I'm dying," he told his wife. "Two or three months the doctor gave me."

Even though he felt chilly he wanted to push open a window. It seemed as though a mist had settled in the apartment. All at once his knees were shaking and bumping each other so violently that his legs nearly buckled. Panicky, his wife stumbled across the room towards him—hung back, paralyzed, not knowing what to do—then abruptly flung her arms around him. He broke her grip, thrusting her away angrily. Then just as suddenly he got hold of himself and apologized. Stiffly, he sat down at the dining room table, indicating a chair for her, and began going over the details of their medical insurance policy.

"Come to bed."
"I'm reading."
"Come to bed. It's late."

He was sitting in the armchair in the living room, browsing through an old detective novel, when the humorous description of an extortionist's death suddenly made him laugh so hard he had to put the book down. He pondered for a few seconds. His hand reached toward the novel, then withdrew quickly. He wanted something to look forward to. At last he rose and went into the bedroom.

When he woke shortly after dawn, he rolled over and looked out through the drizzle. The street lamps were still lit. He lay back down and tried to compose his waking thoughts, then raised himself for another look. Just then the street lamps went out, startling him. He sat straight up and closed his eyes. *Why hadn't it occurred to him before?* . . . What if his wife, obsessed with her grief, were already in mourning? . . . and if he, from some unobserved vantage point, could watch her? . . . and likewise visit the cemetery and look at all the flowers that had been placed over his grave—so many that they hid the stone!

By this, he did not mean that he would visit the world from the afterlife; no, he meant he would recreate the stage scenery of death *before* he died, as a sort of prologue—the black apparel, the bouquets of roses, the widow's adjusted regimen, the speech to fit the new circumstances—so that the fiction might recreate the reality, so that he himself might actually long for the days immediately following his death, those days whose overwhelming sadness had been testimony to how much he had been missed. He would possess *fond memories* of those days.

When he entered the dining room his wife, already seated, was reading the paper as usual. She looked up and asked if he had slept well. That, too, was perfectly normal. But the way she looked at him . . .

He began talking in a measured tone, slowly at first, and without looking at her. It was quite ordinary talk—about fears, the necessary arrangements, providing for her and so forth—but gradually, by degrees, he began dropping in remarks: "And what if one were to do that . . ."; "And just suppose one were to start acting in this manner, admittedly a bit unusual . . ."

He drove alone to a gravestone yard on the edge of the city. Opening the car door, he spread his black umbrella before him, then climbed out and walked over to the little house where he peered through the dim window. A melancholy little man sat inside behind a cluttered desk, with an electric heater on the floor. The man, who turned out to be the owner, looked up, then reached for his own umbrella and joined him outside in the rain.

As the two men walked through the long rows of gravestones, their umbrellas occasionally bumping, they talked as though they were old friends. The owner explained there were a large number of inscriptions to choose from, ranging in price in accordance with the length of the inscription, to which the man replied that, having once been a teacher who assigned essays of such and such number of words, he understood him perfectly.

Soon, the man selected a gravestone, a rather large one. For several minutes they stood side by side before the stone, with the rain drumming lightly on their umbrellas. It was as though someone close to both of them had been buried there.

Beneath a smoke gray sky the car traveled still farther out, climbing up through the sweeping forests that blanketed the low mountains surrounding the city. From the cemetery the man could barely see the downtown buildings—rain clouds had descended, veiling the distant city in mist and drizzle. He found the family plot easily enough; there was a pond beside it, with a stand of firs behind. For a long time he simply stood there, trying to feel comfortable. Eventually, he turned and left.

The rain was falling gently on the city. The man drove carefully through the streets, now choked with rush hour traffic, but as he braked for a light the car suddenly skidded, forcing a shiny yellow taxi, horn blasting, driver shaking his fist out the window, to swerve and climb a sidewalk. Trembling, he pulled over: *bright yellow rain slickers, how it was, how it might have been . . .*

"I was almost killed," he said aloud, then stopped and sat very still. After a while he began to speak again, slowly this time, and more thoughtfully: "The man, who had once been a school teacher, was almost killed by a wet yellow taxi whose color reminded him of . . ."

His wife wore black around the house but wouldn't wear it on the street. That was all right, he didn't press her. But he did finally bring enough pressure to bear so that one cold bright morning she accompanied him to the cemetery where he then shot several rolls of film of her kneeling at the grave site where his coffin had been lowered into the earth on that cold bright morning when a hundred mourners had stood round knee-deep in the snow, heads bowed, hands clasped . . .

At home, thumbing through the photo album:
The widow on her knees at the grave side, her face through blown hair—
Then again, walking along the beach at dusk, the terns running back and forth with the waves—

And what if one were to live one's life in such a way (he speculated) that one's very words could be depended upon to express, at any given moment, whether one were really oneself or someone else, alive or dead, making do with the routine realities, or with the creative fiction of one's death, so that one's very language became an instrument for cutting and sharpening and smoothing out reality, so that all tenses—the past, the present, and the future, all simples, progressives, and perfects—so that all of them dissolved into a mystical contemporaneity of time which traveled, at will, backwards and forwards, up and down, reflecting across its inner chasms every angle and curve of one's life, and everything before, and everything after . . .

"Dear," he said one evening, just after his wife had stepped in the door with a bag of groceries, "you haven't made the casserole for several weeks now."

He did not seem to hear her catch her breath, nor did he look up at her, at least not until she had turned her back and begun arranging the perishables inside the refrigerator. "Yes," she said finally, "he always did like it so much. Now I have to make just enough for myself. But I can't bring myself to do that just yet. It's a comfort to pretend he's still here."

When dinner was ready she sat down at the table with a plate for herself. The man rose from the armchair, which had been moved from the living room into a corner of the dining room, and served himself.

"I will get used to his not being here," she said.

"Yes, he would've understood," the man said, then returned to the armchair where he watched the woman eat supper alone. Her hair was gray, her face was gaunt: she was staring out the window in confusion.

Burghild Holzer

ALIEN TALK

to you it is interesting
voices from other countries
living in the midst of you,
you remember and you tell us
that your neighbor also spoke with that nice accent
to you I am interesting, a voice from Europe
to you it is foreign, a little exotic
                     but to me it is   it is where
    my mother lives, it is where my father is dying, now,
    it is where the graves are open
                    to me it is, Omsale ich hab
    Pfingstrosen im Zimmer und du kannst sie nicht sehen
you call it ethnic, you think of picture books, you think
of your ancestors coming across that ocean
    but you do not know the pain they suffered remembering
    how the rain smelled on the other side of the world
    how grandmother waved and waved in the train station
you say the countryside is beautiful there, you say you
travelled through
                    I write, heute regnet es
    aber es riecht nicht wie bei dir im Garten, es riecht
    nicht wie bei dir
you want to look up your relatives when you are over there
                    but I think of grandmother's
    face under the rosebush under the black stone, I think,
    warum hab ich sie allein gelassen, sie sterben alle und
    ich bin nicht dort
you ask, why did you come here
                    and I shut my mouth in anguish,
    like your ancestor who came across that ocean I cannot
    explain to you the darkness, the fear that pushed me
    forward, the needs that brought me across
you say, why don't you go back
                  and like your ancestors I
    remain silent, cannot show the paths blocked, the faces
    dead
                like your ancestors I turn
  inward, alone with my memories
               like them I watch what I say

            lest you might ask
why don't you go back
                        like them I talk to myself,
      I whisper Omsale, heute im Garten, ein Vogel, fast wie
      eine Amsel im Frühling

 line 11:
*to me it is, Omsale (a loving name for grandmother) I have
peonies in my room and you cannot see them*

 line 20:
*I write, today it is raining
but it does not smell like it does in your garden, it does
not smell like it does at your place*

 line 25:
*I think
why have I forsaken her, they are all dying and
I am not there*

 line 43:
*I whisper Omsale, today in the garden, a bird, almost like
a blackbird in spring*

Bruce Boston

WITHIN THE DIVISIVENESS OF SELF,
ARMIES RANGE

Within the divisiveness of self disembodied arms
hurl silver balls along the uneven greens,
armies range, and some old gaffer with an eyepatch
wants to know the score. There is a purity in the
flatness of his vision which belies gradation.
As ballistas of the heart unleash their fury
he waits, his arms full of treaties and chess sets,
his single eye blinking like a beacon. By night
he trods the fields, pushing pins into mountaintops.
Like a circuit judge he roams the dark highway,
jouncing in the saddle, tamping down the dawn
with his gavel. The clenched universe unwinds, night
grades to day. Yes or no? he cries in his cloven voice,
but the pins keep flying across a shattered landscape
where armies range and small animals cluster,
where every face imaginable offers its eyes
to the changing, changing light.

THE ALCHEMIST IS BORN
IN A SUDDEN CHANGING OF SEASONS

Each winter morning,
bare and heavy,
apprenticed to the fires
of the smithy's shop,
I bore my trade upon my back.
I forged my soul to cooling metals.

Plangently the hammer would ring
in the day's first stillness,
loud against a chalky sun,
sending the wrens to higher perches
in the oaks and sycamores,
the deserted reaches of the barn.

These blows would shake my teeth,
drop sparks about my ankles

and singe the hair
upon my turning arms.
Each falling arc trembled
the air in its breaking.

One day I watched the sun
drift north, bright as my furnace.
The snow had fled the gables,
and by the morning roadside,
soft crucibles of gold
opened among the leaves.

Climbing to the loft
I was pinned, left speechless.
There in darkness,
pale as old straw,
the pulsing throat
of a bird I could not name.

BREATH FALLS AND IS NOT STONE

Sensing at last that the voice
of the soul is not the eyes,
but the lines beneath them,
this map of falling flesh,
I cover these streets,
footfalls on voiceless stone.
I think of Rodin, the bright windows,
the statues in the high room,
of stone about to speak.

Somewhere, lover, you lie,
senses disarrayed,
stoned dreams upon the brain,
the streets beneath your eyes
softened by sleep. If I listen,
I can hear you breathing,
each breath a weightless tone
which rises from your lips.

At dawn in the alleyway I wait.
Light descends like a plumbline,
breath falls and is not caught.
You awaken beyond the dream,

turn back the sheets,
step within the lines of day.
Your eyes, like mine, are squinting,
so crinkled against this brightness.

WOMAN ON THE STATION PLATFORM
for Anna Kavan
British novelist, 1904-68

The chill was leaving her body.
All night, wincing through the downpour,
she had watched the rains thin.

Her coat was windflapped,
alive with the smell of its wetness.

By dawn the clouds had fallen.
She saw the last stars
burning
unaltered
before each disappeared
in the surrounding brightness.

TOUCHSTONE

When the music played
summer was a veil
upon the streets.
He opened the doors
to let the notes
slide across the lawn.
Staffs brushing the grasses,
furrowing the dry earth,
until they reached the walk
and began pulling at the people.
And the people came into the house,
with hats and without,
laughing.

The note hangs suspended.
Visualize a droplet
with a fluted tail
sailing

ready to burst upon the ear.
Reverse the tape and listen.
The silence before birth
is all at once.

When winter came
and the world went white
he took the projector
onto the icy lawn,
a black extension cord
winding up and back
and through the lighted window.
Against the walls of snow
he ran a film of summer:
leaves and dogs
and the freshly cut grasses
and the people filling the house
with music.

REPORT FROM NICOLAS

he trudged into the wilderness
seeking the god whose words
are weaved in wood, his back pack
like a steely carapace
shielding him from the sun

he joined the serried grasses
of the field in their slow green
war of survival and destruction

he sent us letters, etched
with a stubby pencil, printed
because we could not read his writing,
a loose plenum of graphite bones
treading the white water of the page

he wrote that he was trying to live *a terre*
like the king who spends his life in the saddle

he wrote that he was dedicating himself
to the transcription of realities

he wrote that he was weary of "endless
first person confessionals wrung from
the pistils of wilting flower souls"

in his free moments he would collect
metaphors like beanbags and toss them
about
     "the ribs of the earth bunch together"
     "mountains gather like lowing cattle"
     "the sun is a great golden cock and
       the moon, the pale abyss of an empty womb"

he formed phrases like freshly bought
candles, their wicks still clean,
calling them sutras rather than maxims
since he liked the eastern flavor of the
word
     "breath falls from the lungs and is not caught"
     "it takes more than two legs to leave"
     "the rain does not choose the forest or the plain"

from the ashen and igneous earth
he excavated melted glass bottles,
decanters, demijohns, forgotten figurines

in the high grasses he lay like a planchet
awaiting the stamp of whatever realm would
claim him first, to be spent accordingly
on boots wine tallow or mutton

in his dreams he was a hard kernel
of a man, no meat within the seed

in his dreams he was a meaty man
with love flourishing in his soul

in his nightmares, from the dizzying height
of the falcon's aerie, a host of many-footed
symbols came rushing toward him, furry and junctured
and carrying flags, a youth with the wings of
a bat, a meniscus moon, a japanese dagger,
a broken bird, an old man with fool's gold
in the pinks of his eyes . . . . .

he wrote that by summer his money would be gone
and he would travel south with the sun
to sleep on the warm beaches among the mottled shells,
to mix among the dark races and drink their strong beer
and laugh with dark laughter for their women
until the moon was replete and brimming

the rain does not choose the forest or the plain,
the tiger does not know that it is tiger named

SHORT CIRCUITS
(from a longer manuscript of the same title)

Romanticism Has Forgotten How To Fly

From the cantilevered balconies of Pamplona the yellow ladies throw roses hairy with thorns. Bullfighters catch them in their teeth, and lips bleeding, rampage the narrow streets. They are on their way to the arena and as the first arrives he casts open the gates and charges the bull. He grabs the horns and is about to wrestle the beast to its knees when . . . metamorphosis ? . . . it is transformed into a giant aluminum can.

The other men enter the arena. They tip the can onto its side and begin rolling it about, but there is no way to puncture the top. They hear a thumping from within. They back away as the metal begins to crackle. Rimples appear in its once-sleek surface. A leather wing. A horned foot. The metal shears and a massive pterodactyl stumbles forth, belches once, and collapses upon the sand.

Stretching the body spread-eagle, the men lower their nets and begin staking out its hide. All about them, tier upon tier, the stadium is empty. And above, in the perfect circle of the sky: no clouds.

Separate Vacations

A husband and wife decided to take separate vacations. After two weeks the husband returned, but his wife had not arrived. Over the next week she began to come back to him, piece by piece. On Tuesday a brown paper package arrived containing her laugh and her left ear. Two days later, a shoebox with her feet. On Friday, a manila envelope with a few locks of hair and the nape of her neck. On Saturday, a breast with a dark brown nipple. Yet the following Monday, and over the whole next week, nothing.

The pieces of the wife are stacked in the corner. The husband waits each day in silence for the sturdy click of the post lady's heels, the hinges on the metal box. He has begun to hear strange rumors about the mail service. Stories of mechanized sorting plants where boxes are mutilated, of packages being delivered to incorrect addresses or lying in freight cars on abandoned railroad sidings. And now when he looks to the corner of the room he begins to wonder if that is really his wife's breast.

Discoveries

The pond is sheltered by a bower of trees. The mirror of its surface is obscured by algae and stinking leaves; its depths are murky with silt. Yet this is where I discover the gold. Not dust, but nuggets. Raw and brilliant as the sun.

I run back up the path to the house to tell Marie. I find her hiding naked in the closet.

"What the hell!" I exclaim.

"They're after me again."

"Who?"

"The bats," she wails. "The spiders. The telephone poles!"

Grabbing her by the ears I haul her onto the carpet. "Look, you fool! Gold!"

I hurl the nuggets against the wall and they splatter like paint and begin to dribble down the paper. Marie hurries over and sucks up each droplet before it can reach the floor. She turns and stands and takes off her nakedness. Where are the buttons, I wonder, as she begins to dance in her bones.

We Build a Better Pet

A turtle, nothing special, a grayish green turtle wearing an equally grayish green shell with a few lumps on it, a turtle named Mark belonging to J.R. Salton of Santa Monica, Ca., was run over by a United Parcel van on Wilshire Blvd. Scraped off the asphalt still flickering with life Mark was rushed to UCLA Medical Center where a covey of ace veterinarians, using copper wire, the salvage from a '48 Piper Cub and the brain of a chicken, created the first bionic reptile . . . MARK TWO.

No fairy tales, this tortoise *can* outrace the hare.

He can jump five feet into the air to catch flies. When the moon is new and the corn is ripe he can do a reasonable impression of mezzo soprano Joan Ditto. And he looks just like any other turtle. Except for the rivets in his head.

The Needles Tracking

Too rapidly the dots accumulate. Dr. Spoleri adjusts the electrodes. He thumbs his glasses and calculates the nation. He is something more than a doctor, less than a man of medicine. In the lumpy geography of his soul the vision of an endless city blooms by night.

Its streets are empty, its houses full.

The doctor nudges a toggle and the juices begin to flow. Distance is pressed to a simple line, the tongue of a blade, the oval lip of a freshly coined bullet. Trapped by a dark geometry of wires, spirits are tapped to the core. Hands jerk and touch. Strange creatures spawn. Dr. Spoleri cuffs his knuckles on the motor mount and curses the dawn. He is Swiss and claims neutrality. The moons of his glasses fill with light. There are a million threads in his jacket, a million upon a million, all of them running blood.

SOLDIER, SAILOR

Death is as ordinary and natural as any event, and murder hardly less so. If I kill a man in the woods there is no need for the city to know. My long stride carries me far through the breadth of the night and by sunrise there is no longer moss beneath my feet but the fog-slickened cobbles of a port metropolis. I make my way past the shuttered morning houses and dead shop windows, down to the harbour and along the wooden quays. I pitch my country cap at a jaunty angle and walk with a roll upon the balls of my feet. The seasoned boards creak beneath. The salty dawn braces my lungs as I survey the resting ships. Making my way back to the town proper I find a sailors' bar and there I drink my beer.

And what of the woods?

I have never been to the woods. Now I am a sailor with the bristle of the sea air still spiking each exhalation of my breathing. That is my ship moored in the harbour, The Queen Marie, that white beauty with the polished silver scuppers and the tall masts pitched to the line of her movement. That streamlined beauty, a proud ship to serve and I have served her well to earn my space of rest from the wave roar and water roll which have limited the dimensions of my movements for months. The country? The woods? Yes, perhaps I would like to go someday, yet I am a sailor and my seaworthy feet might feel ill-at-ease with nothing but the morose solidity of the land unfolding from them in all directions as far as my spyglass could see. My hands would no doubt grow restless with no ropes to hold. Those hardy broad-beamed country girls would seem strange pale creatures to me after the learned and desolate women of these port cities. And now I have snuffed out two consciousnesses in those woods, that other and my own past self.

. . . .

Of course what really matters is that I never meant to kill him in the first place. There was no conscious intention, no . . . . ah . . . . premeditation is what they choose to label it in the courts of law. Only . . . . hmn . . . . technically could you clip the tag "MURDERER" to my collar and place my mug staring grimly out of focus from some government wall. It all began as a harmless scuffle, a difference of opinion. Even less, a mere misunderstanding over a few copper coins or a woman or politics or the weather—nothing more than that. You must realize that he came at me first. I myself am not a man of passion, not even a very sexual man. I have always concerned myself with the business of life rather than its pastimes. My nature is normally docile, well-controlled. My brow is unseamed by creases of tension or strife; my face translucent, without guile. But not him! He was a threatening fellow from the very start, no doubt of that, a dangerous rogue with that raw-boned lantern jaw of his and those hunching shoulders. He was an ugly man. Physically ugly! Who is to say afterall? It may well be that I have done the world a service, eliminated a beast who could only bring unhappiness and suffering to all those about him. And what of . . . . circumstances?! In spite of what the law courts preach you can forget that fiction about individual responsibility. Quite the contrary. All of us are but the quarry of our circumstances. Thus you see that it could have happened to anyone. It could just as well have been the other way round and he could have been the one to have left me in the forest with my back impaled upon a rock and the cold claiming my bones, with treacly dewdrops of blood gathered about my lips, my clothing dew-damp to the touch, the weeds growing with my hair, my nails still growing night and day until they found me or whatever tattered cloth and bone remains the animals had left of me. And if it had been such would he have claimed his modicum of guilt any more readily than I?

· · · ·

It is McCauley who is going to teach me. I encountered him last night during the final rounds of an evening-long drinking bout. He says that I am going to make a fine sailor . . . . ah yes, a veritable model of the sea. Already he has procured my togs for me from the locker of a dead mate, the well-worn shirts and belled breeches which mark my experience as a professional. They fit me handsomely and I have been aware of more than one woman glancing my way in the crowded streets of this port city.

McCauley himself, though a bit old, is all right—except for his excessive drinking and his dank breath and his aversion to the daylight. He claims that the land sun is a different sort of animal altogether than the sea sun, that it drys the marrow out of one's bones and saps one's virility. Consequently, while ashore he spends the major portion of the daytime hours in a bar, a sailors' bar of course—low-ceilinged, drafty, with rugged sneezing whores, the smell of pitch and fish and damp tobacco, and other sailor smells to which I have yet to grow accustomed. He leans toward me conspiratorially over our beers and I have to hold my own breathing to avoid the smell of his.

"A sailor's life is a good life," he tells me, as he has told me before, "a life of freedom on the open seas with no country to bind you. Whenever you want you can settle down for awhile in a port and live a little." He gives me a sort of wink and the wrinkles of his face, more wrinkles than his age should provide, scrunch about in a spastic dance as his features re-arrange themselves. "And if your papers are in order you can always find a new berth. The only bad thing is those damn gay boys—it draws them like flies to honey!" His small eyes dance meanly around the room as if ferreting out the presence of any of the accursed "gay boys." "Of course all you have to do is straighten them out from the start if they give you any of their shit!" He chops the edge of his callused palm against the wooden bar rail and offers his most malicious grin.

The old fool is probably a queer himself and a sadist to boot—whether he's willing to admit it or not, whether he even knows it or not.

· · · ·

"Murder"—to some a delicious word, to most an abomination. For certain it does not fall easily from the tongue. For certain it is no simple dissyllable. An "oven" can be open or shut. It can bake a potato or broil a roast. A "bottle" can be full or empty. Full, it can quench one's thirst; empty, it can serve as a ready club. Ah, but a "murder," past, present, or future, (to paraphrase McCauley) is a different sort of animal altogether. For some an obsession, for others a compulsion, it can set its tentacles in the mind with unbending intent. It can leave blood in the street and money rotting in the bank, lay the healthy man in his grave, take husband from wife or wife from husband, abate the heat of passion and leave lovers turning cold and blue in one another's arms. In the plural, as it is often practiced, it can topple empires and cause new ones to rise up in their places with corpses aplenty as solid foundation stones. It can send one man to prison while another man, it can fill his chest with medals and his soul with flak. Being involved in the death of a fellow human being can be an intense experience. Perhaps it might give a man, even an heretical man, a faith.

. . . .

I am waiting in a city by the sea. In a port city my mind is facing the fields, the hills, the woods and I do not know if the sea behind me is devouring the land or only kissing it. I am waiting for the sea to kiss and devour me. I am dancing in a city by the sea and I am more than a little drunk. Above me the ambulatory stars are passing in a cycle I do not understand. All about me the whores are laughing; the lights, gay and electric, are dying for the night; the city is preparing for its rest. Beside me a dank man with too many tattoos is emptying himself one by one of the dank episodes of his life. He lays them out like overchewed tobacco plugs. He lays them out like the empty beer mugs sitting before us. Tonight they will be washed and tomorrow re-appear clean and face down upon the shelf behind the bar, ready for the following evening's diversion and amusement.

McCauley is my unflagging companion these days—I have little choice in the matter until he obtains the identification papers for me he has promised with such certitude. Each morning I meet him by the harbour and as we make our daily tour of inspection he imparts to me a bit of his professionalism and a good deal of his nonsense. Clippers, frigates, schooners, sloops, topsails, fore, main and mizzen masts, half-hitches, reeve knots, figures-of-eight, bow-lines—I am learning them all, and inevitably learning McCauley in the process. It is for certain that in moments of need or anxiety one can be too ready to fasten upon particular companions. The man is even less desirable than I had at first imagined. Now his various faults—physical, mental, emotional—become more and more apparent. Although he has inhabited the ever-changing sea for so long, he himself has become set and changeless in his ways, the skeleton of his mind as rigid as any crustacean. Despite all of his travels, in his own way he is as petty as any small town burgher, as superstitious as any fishwife. McCauley's world is a tightrope world, jointly inhabited by black and white men, up and down signposts, a world where all question marks have been banished, buried and forgotten. As he walks along the quays he lays out his formulations, haphazard and pedantic. You can mark a man by the worth of his calluses (I feel my own learned and lily palms self-consciously). A southerly wind blows no good. A sailor's life is a good life except for the damn gay boys. One, two, three—they are inked as clearly as his unfading tattoos, they peal incessantly against the sky of his personal reality, a sky so low with horizon so abridged it could be no more than an overturned egg cup. And as we walk he exclamates the tenets of this credenda with an obsessive cough, barking up thick pellets of mucous from his speckled throat as the thinning cords of his neck jump to attention with each sharp report. One, two three!—into the harbour water they go. There is so much human debris and garbage afloat there already that McCauley's contribution, even if tubercular, will have little effect.

We order lunch, grease-logged fish and potatoes at one of the open air shops along the quay, and then eat with our feet dangling over the pier edge as the dreary water laps sluggishly about below us. (I have found the explanation for McCauley's foul saline breath: though you'd think he'd be sick of it by now, fish is practically all he eats.) Afterwards, with my companion's steps hastening to salvage his drying marrow and waning virility from the onslaught of the afternoon sun, we head up to The Longman for beer after beer, to grow increasingly bilious throughout the long, dull and bilious afternoon. One by one the girls tumble downstairs or in off the street, frowsy and disheveled, yawning away to bare their uneven teeth, a shiny gold-capping here, an open pink-soled chasm there, perhaps where a patron, too hearty or drunk or dissatisfied, has knocked them about. I wonder if each man they have been with has not left his mark, of one sort or another, upon them. Of course all of these women have something wrong with them, there is something awry, either in their external physiognomies or the physiognomies of their souls, or they would never be sailors' whores in the first place. Marie has a crooked mouth. Lily, though young enough, is hollow-cheeked with her features pinched by a chloritic tinge. The old one they call "Doll," beneath her palimpsest of paint and paste, is as leathery as any steer. Such an unsavory collection of females it has seldom been my misfortune to purvey. Still, I do not doubt that on occasions of passion some are serviceable enough. And I must admit that I have not been unaware, particularly in my moments of drunkeness, of a saving grace here or there—a shapely pair of calves or a large well-rounded breast resting lightly against the wooden rail of the bar. McCauley knows them all (they call him "Mac") and will often send one on her way with a jocund swat across the butt. He even enumerates their faults and favors to me, ticking them off one by one on his wirey, insensate paws, though he never seems to partake of the fare. In truth, he has more covetous eyes for young Alan, the barman's son who waits table, and who in turn eyes a few of the more nubile girls with tender fright. At this point the youth's incipient manhood has only burgeoned sufficiently to raise a constricting lump in his throat, and it is no doubt this boyishness which attracts McCauley.

Throughout all of our evenings of drinking (and they seem to accumulate so rapidly) I have observed that McCauley, in spite of the quantity of our consumption, never lets it get the better of him. Beneath a dross veil of drunkenness he always maintains the upper hand. At some level, as he winds out his worn tales and exoteric opinions, he remains lucid and calculating. I am less careful, for I can only tolerate the tedium of his companionship when a bit of bacchus has joined our duo. As the weight of the evening lies more heavily upon me, I betray my country origins by ordering and drinking wine. Then the unoccupied whores pull me, always at first unwillingly, into turning dances. Drawn in at the peripheries, I become lost in heated conversations with wayfaring strangers. I laugh at sailor's jokes I do not understand and exchange, one for one, hearty slaps upon the back. Yet suddenly, in the midst of a dance or a drink or a laugh, the strangeness of my surroundings reimpresses itself upon me and I no longer mistake the alcoholic ruddiness in those unfamiliar faces for warmth. In a fit of *mal du pays* I sink back down to my post beside McCauley. With maudlin concentration I silently weep for my lost home, my lost past.

On some nights my "friend" has to rouse me from our table and help me bodily to the room I have taken upstairs—with too eager a hand so that I half-expect him to snatch my purse or attempt to seduce me. Yet so far, he merely guides me to bed and tucks me in with the ministering professionalism of a manservant. Then he departs to carry on the night alone. Sleep claims my drunkenness, my homelessness, my knowledge and my guilt. Above me the stars continue to pass. They understand that I never meant to kill him. The whores know that I am not a man of passion. Bacchus, shrunk to the dimensions of a cherub, plays a lullaby-fiddle on my right shoulder. The city sleeps without knowledge of my crime and somewhere in the night streets, amidst the ambient coast fog, on this lip of the land above the devouring sea, McCauley with all the deftness of a beggar-blindman, is tapping out the trail to my identification papers.

. . . .

If one lived here for years on end one might fill this room with the desserts of one's days. It could become as comfortable as an old jacket, as secure and certain in defining one's identity as the well-marked skin of certain caterpillars. Instead, it has been filled by chance with the odds and ends of a hundred different lives. The barman and innkeeper has proven enterprising enough so that with the aid of his sailor connections (perhaps even McCauley's aid) he has long since obtained the concession for storing unclaimed cargoes in his ample cellar. By something more than chance alone these objects have tended to gravitate upstairs to furnish and over-furnish the rooms of the inn. I understand that more than once a sleeping guest has had to be awakened in the night to retrieve a particular valuable, no longer in mint condition, whose rightful owner had suddenly materialized in most unwanted fashion. My single chamber alone offers a patchwork of the world beyond the sea, of large objects and small, of good taste and bad commingled to a tasteless jumble easily as happenstance and varied as McCauley's tattoos or the whores below. The intended destinations of these objects are now as lost as the objects themselves, though in many cases their points of origin can still be deduced. Whatever their genesis, they have come to rest here. The wallpaper for instance (sloppily affixed above the worn wood paneling) with its mock trellis and vine flowering highly stylized *fleur-de-lis* I take to be of French origin, as I do the dark walnut escritoire with its curved provincial lines, now badly scarred. Perchance these were once intended for the country study of some rich merchant who, during the lengthy passage of his purchases, left his life behind or had it taken from him. The sofa is British, a prehistoric blue velvet Chesterfield with rising springs and loose batting escaping to the four corners of the room, to skitter beneath the bed where no one, chambermaid included, is industrious to retrieve it. The bed itself is a Colonial four-poster once meant to uphold a canopy which no doubt has found an equally unlikely home elsewhere. The clock above the mantle is one of those Swiss monstrosities with a turning platform sporting tiny figures in leather shorts and tyrolean hats who celebrate the hour on the hour—fortunately the mechanism is either broken or disconnected, leaving the celebrants in mid-spin, frozen as woodenly as their substance. No single individual could have brought all of these objects together with any conception of a decorous whole; no one is that unpredictable or that complex.

But I must not forget the mirror. Every room needs a mirror in which to reflect itself. This one, perched incongruously atop a high dresser, is a child's fairy tale mirror, oval with fake gold lamé trim. Still its glass is true and finely silvered. Within it, the room repeats its mismatched identity. Within it my reflection is perfect, as unspoiled as the sunlight: the receding shock of sandy hair, now badly in need of a cutting; the low features, always blander than I envision them in my mind's eye, always older than I remember them; the flat cheeks and rounded chin; the grey eyes with just a hint of dishonesty about the corners. I tick off the faults and favors of this face against the insensate walls. It could be a murderer's face. It could be the face of a learned man or a fool, a liar, a hypocrite, a man of many minor passions, a man of virtues unlimited.

. . . .

The truth of the matter is that one kills things all the time, often without even knowing it. Do not certain doctors tell us of the micro-organisms we send down the drain to oblivion with each mere washing of our hands? Have you never walked a night road after the rain and felt with a twinge of slight remorse the helpless bodies of unseen snails crunching beneath your boots? And what of the leather in those boots, once living flesh, or the meat upon our tables? I dare say even the vegetables we consume—as growing plants they no doubt possessed life to some degree and perhaps some slow seeping consciousness. Who is to judge the worth of this consciousness or that, the value of this life or that death? Who is to punish or absolve? The high court judge with his black robes and powdered wig? The pecuniary voice of the newspapers? That avaricious mass called "the people" and oft-glorified with a capital "P"? I say better that there be no judgment at all than such brands of madness as these. Or better yet, that each man explore his own inner self and serve as his own judge, jury and even executioner if the need be.

. . . .

The Bathysphere is the lone tourist attraction of this harbour, imported piecemeal from Lubeck and assembled locally at no meagre cost. Still, for a reasonable admittance fee, one can descend with others in a hermetically sealed diving bell and from behind the security of double plate glass view what are billed as "The Strange Mysteries of the Underwater World." If one were actually viewing the normal depths of these shoreline waters the only mysteries to be seen would be a lot of barnacles, a few sickly pike or cod, an occasional water snake and a good deal of algae. In consequence, they have cordoned off a small portion of the bay with netting and stocked it with mysteries ready-made, underwater enough yet hardly endemic.

At first I had trouble convincing McCauley to break from our daily routine and go down in the Bathysphere, and even once he consented his anxiety was apparent. While sealed within and descending his stringy muscles began to tense, his knuckles whiten. A neat coating of sweat beaded upon his temples and upper lip and looked to be a cold sweating. I realized that he had probably seen the briney swallow enough men for keeps so that he fears its depths mightily. By the time we reached bottom his usual blind buoyancy had deserted him completely: his very tattoos seemed to writhe. The plenteous assortment of marine life billowing about us failed to involve him sufficiently so that he could forget his plight, namely, that although bone-dry he was beneath the waves rather than atop them. It was not until several minutes after we surfaced and were once again on solid earth that he reverted to his normal, splenetic self.

But what did we see below . . . . .

Against a landscaped background of spidery white anemones and pink coral the underwater menagerie gathered about our bell. As a suited diver ventured forth to feed them, our guide delineated the attractions: colorful clown fish, sand-burrowing flounders, a small male leopard shark with its less brilliantly shaded mate, a school of pale albino cichlids swimming in perfect unison, a black and white turkey fish, its multiple fins rippling sinuously like whores' plumage, a baby octopus, a giant grouper which came close to the glass and seemed to stare back at us with dull soporific amazement. In truth, all of the creatures in this netherworld are fed constantly so that they are bloated and tranquilized, stuffed nearly to the point of sedation. Otherwise, with such crowding they must perforce turn upon one another in a grand spectacle of subaqueous carnage, tearing fins, rending gills and gullets, churning the water blood-turbid, devouring, killing . . . . murdering.

. . . .

The identification papers, that's the rub. If it were a mere question of money there would be no question at all, for I must admit in retrospect that my accident, my misdeed, my crime, call it what you will, netted me more than a few copper coins. Not that that was the reason mind you, but afterall, money is of no use to a dead man and why should I have left it for whoever found the body or for some local officials to pocket and divy up. In any case, as the eager whores have oft-noticed, my purse is full. Still, it is not a mere question of money and McCauley has explained this to me again and again in utmost detail, for it is truly a detailed subject. First, if I am to leave the country, there is the problem of both a passport and visa. The latter can be forged from scratch, yet to forge the former one must first obtain a passport booklet which needs to come directly from a district capital. Furthermore, if I am to leave in the role of an employed seaman I will need merchantman's papers, a union card, a dues card paid to date, and a credible employment record which cannot be double-checked. On top of all this are the standard identification papers required of all citizens: birth certificate, registry papers, medical cards, etc. Of all these numerous papers, cards, and booklets, some can be forged, some stolen, some "happened upon" in ways about which McCauley is not willing to elaborate. Thus more than mere money it all boils down to a question of time, patience and chance. Yet as the time accumulates, my patience wears thin, and chance, as always, is just as likely to fall against one as for. In my most nightmarish imaginings the blue-cuffed hand of authority, rapacious, clamps down upon my shoulder just as I am mounting the gangplank to depart for my glorious life of freedom on the open seas—and McCauley, a suddenly anonymous seaman, turns his head away as if he has never known me.

· · · ·

Well, I finally gave in to one last night. It was Lily, the one with the calves (and thighs and body to match I discovered). Afterall, even the most moderate man needs an occasional diversion, an amusement, however minor, to relieve the tedium of such unresolved waiting. Besides, it allowed me to escape McCauley a bit earlier in the evening.

She turned out to be different, more perceptive than I'd expected. As she ran her clever fingers about my wrist and palm she told me, "You're not like most sailors, you're more tender . . . . more . . . . afraid."

"What am I then?" I asked her with a chuckle.

She looked at me wide-eyed, her expression a mix of gravity and suspense. "That I wouldn't know, for beyond sailors I have no knowledge of other men."

There were other ways in which she surprised me, also. I picked her for her girlishness—and on the one hand she is girlish. Yet on the other hand, she's a professional *par excellence*. She can't have been a whore for more than a few years, but I suppose as in most professions, that's all it takes to pick up the tricks of the trade. In any case, once she saw the glitter of my gold (or is that unfair?) she unleashed her complete repertoire and played across my body as if I were a fine fiddle. Her tongue alone had long-mastered the arts of excitation, not to mention her hands and limbs and the animal cunning and abandon (feigned?) of her small tight body. Beneath the expertise of her touch I became lost and locked in the grip of a sexuality so intense that it consumed all my conscious thought, all conscious control. And after I emptied myself into her, trembling, spasmodic, crying out and unable to stop, my thoughts emerged again only gradually, drifting up through a soft, slack semi-awareness in which I felt as much gutted as sated.

Afterwards, for I bought her for the duration of the night, she prepared and lit a long pipe for me and we smoked and talked together, nearly like lovers. The pungent smoke soon filled our heads and the room, draping its distorting veil about the furnishings. For a moment they took on different proportions and faces and all seemed to match. They became the bizarre trappings of my private seraglio and I was ensconced like some oriental despot, in royal splendor with my latest bride. The revelry which penetrated from the tavern below was no more than the celebrating guests of our nuptial feast, drinking to my continued health and prosperity.

"I'm glad to be here with you rather than downstairs," Lily told me.

"Why?"

"Because it's quiet here and you're different than the others. You only ask of me what I am willing to give."

Before sleep took us we locked again—at her initiative! Either she was determined to give me my money's worth in the hopes of the request for a repeat performance or she actually is drawn to me. The second time was no less intense than the first and I swear that when I came she was right there with me!

Perchance I could forget my thoughts of becoming a sailor and stay here in this city. Lily's still young enough and soft enough so that she could be weaned away from her trade. And what better wife could a man ask for than one already trained in the ways of love? But of course, shades of the opiate are still across my mind, causing me to forget myself. It is not love or even sex which is my leitmotif. Not that I had any choice in the matter, but it is, plain and simple, no more no less than murder.

. . . .

I sensed from the first that this night would be different, just as the day was, only I could not sense how. The difference of the day was the rain. The coast fog held all morning, coalescing to a showering of large droplets just before noon, driving McCauley and myself back up into the town and the tavern early. Those droplets cleansed the dirty city air and left it saturated with their own smell, reminding me of the country. Yet within and beneath that simple odor of the rain I could sense something hiding, more complex, foreboding and different.

The tavern keeper, ever-hospitable and eager for my money, welcomed us as always. The room was already filled with others seeking refuge from the unceasing downpour which was now beating against the leaded glass windowpanes. Behind the iron grate of the fireplace several logs were crackling, and occasionally sizzling as a stray droplet found its way down the voluted chimney and back up again as steam. The whores, pressed into service early, seemed more sleepy and awry than ever yet nonetheless willing to please. Young Alan was waiting table as usual. The entire scene was as normal and pedestrian as could be. Still, something seemed amiss. I sensed it and perhaps McCauley could, too. For one thing, the tether by which we now found ourselves bound—of companionship, of knowledge, of money and the still-hypothetical identification papers—was growing tauter. Both of us were beginning to feel the full force of each tug along the line. Despite all his repetitions, McCauley was running out of things to teach me or tell me. I knew all the seaman's knots, could name the sails as well as he. In consequence, our natural dislike of one another's natures was beginning to surface. Increasingly, I saw him as a preachy old fool; more and more, he saw me as an impatient, unappreciative, young one. The rain had saved us this morning. We were indoors with drink aplenty to take all the edge off our differences. But what would keep us from each other's throats tomorrow or the day after?

Like most other habituates of the tavern we took the rain as an excuse to start drinking earlier and to get more drunk than usual. There was enough of a chill in the air so that our bones needed more warming than beer alone could provide, so McCauley suggested "a true sailor's drinking bout," rum with beer chasers. I acquiesced, the fumes rose quickly from my empty belly, and by mid-afternoon I was thoroughly awash in a mellow and heavy-limbed glow. The stale tobacco smoke which lined the walls of the room borrowed the color of the rum to become a honeyed haze. McCauley was as drunk as I'd ever seen him, and I likewise. At that point, he seemed a capital fellow to me, as good as gold, and Lily's eyes and bare arms pulling me up to dance, her face flushed from her own drinking, seemed far more precious than that. Perhaps another evening with her was in order, I thought as we spun about—abed with Lily by my side and a few puffs of the long pipe and everything would be fine, God in his heaven and all right with the world. After that my continuity began to disintegrate. I remember the tavern door kept opening and closing as more people jammed their way into the packed room, causing those positioned near the entrance to yell out in protest as the cold rain and wind lashed inward. I remember myself and Lily dancing close by that door as it opened with an icy blast against our overheated bodies, afterwards laughing as we shook the clinging droplets from our faces and hair and brushed them from our clothes. I remember McCauley wildly drunk and giving himself away blatantly, laughing from his throat, running his hand up the back of Alan's thigh and over the curve of his buttocks as the youth bent forward trying to hear above the din and take an order at the adjoining table.

Eventually, the quantity of liquor I had consumed overcame me. I must have sunk into a semi-conscious stupor or reverie, for the next thing I knew McCauley was kicking my calf beneath the table to rouse me. The tavern was even more crowded than I recalled, though somewhat less noisy and alive due to the very inhibitions of that crowding. The windowpanes, still rain-speckled but drying, were now black. Outside, dusk had passed and evening arrived without my noticing. A half-emptied mug of beer sat before me, and my bladder, of late overloaded and overworked, was once again calling for relief. McCauley nudged me again.

"Well, lad, you want your identity papers, eh? Well there's your bloody papers," he nodded.

"What?" I answered, still stuporous.

He leaned toward me, bleary-eyed and holding his beer stein, and in too loud a voice shouted close by my ear. "You'll have your papers, lad, we'll take one down tonight. There's your papers, by God, on that very one." The gnarled pointer of McCauley's forefinger directed my eyes to the rear of the tavern, the end of the bar, where through the lamp-yellowed smoke at first I could only make out a covey of older whores clustered together and cackling away in their whores' cacology. Then I noticed a group of seamen standing beyond them. "There," McCauley added with an irascible shaking of his head, "that damn red-headed one! Barry!"

The young sailor whom he apparently meant looked no different to me than a hundred others I had seen in and out of that same room. "You mean he's a forger?" I asked stupidly.

"Barry, a forger!" The joke was uproarious and McCauley couldn't stop laughing, rocking back and forth in his chair with his mean eyes reduced to slits, spilling his beer about the already puddled table. "Why that one's no forger. He's nothing but a damn queer!"

As I stumbled through the crowd to relieve myself I tried to get a better look at this man McCauley had designated as the key to my papers and thus my freedom. I still wasn't thinking clearly and just the effort of standing and walking set my head swimming again. I did manage to get enough of a glimpse to tell that this "Barry" was younger than myself and at least as thoroughly drunk. Above his lineless freckled face his eyes even met mine for a moment, ingenuous and without recognition of any sort.

Within the narrow confines of the privy, temporarily isolated from the chaos beyond, I attempted to bring together my scattered and running thoughts without success. If I had it would have all made sense to me right then, before it was too late. Yet try as I might, I was still totally disordered. As fast as my bladder seemed to be spilling the drink out of me, I had consumed it even faster. The alcohol was still coursing through my veins in potent rivulets which left my limbs glowing, yet heavy. It still saturated my brain to send my thoughts hopping about this way and that, widershins, helterskelter, at random from one cubbyhole to the next like some mad cretin crawling and flinging itself about a checkerboard. Yet never could I rise high enough above the board to perceive the pattern, simple as it was. One second it was thoughts of Lily which transfixed my attention, her image draped across my mind, her tight body, in fantasy, draped snugly about my own. With the next second it was the long-sought identification papers and the release from fear of apprehension which they promised. Then it was a childish fear of water and drowning. I saw myself at sea, washed overboard by a monster wave, devoured by leopard sharks.

If I left with the papers I must leave Lily and leap into the unknown. If I remained it could only be as a fugitive. There was no middle ground and the fog which the rum had packed into my skull refused to coalesce to a cleansing rain of answers. When I emerged once again into the room, still unresolved and wrestling within its tenebrous clutches, the modality of the scene I perceived had changed to accompany my mood. My vision had become as scattered and running as my thoughts. I saw the whores, the tavern keeper, Alan, the sailors, Lily, McCauley—all so many tattoos etched upon the skein of the air and like tattoos slowly puckering with age. I saw them all in my drunkenness, tacky clock toys who at the tolling of the hour would go wheeling into the street *en masse*. I saw them and I wished I had stopped ten drinks before, a hundred drinks before: netherworld creatures, their medium a curdled pudding of lamplight, laughter and smoke, its pellicle, a compost of sex to keep them sated and liquor to keep them tranquilized. I saw them, the People with a capital "P" who, if they knew, would sooner see me gibbeted than raise their glasses with me, and I saw myself moving among them, the unconfessed murderer (yes, murderer!) in flight for his all-too-meagre life. And as I moved through them I felt the pressure of their limbs and bodies locking in catatonic unison against me, demarcating the path I must follow.

I reached the table and turned to begin searching the rear of the bar in vain for the sailor called "Barry."

"The papers," I croaked to McCauley, "the papers!"

"Well come on, you fool, hurry," he bellowed back, "it may already be too late!"

He shoved my coat upon me and began guiding and pushing me through the crush of bodies and toward the door. As we fought our way free and were expelled onto the cobbles outside I turned awkwardly for one last look—of the tavern, of Lily as she was hustled upstairs oblivious to my departure and clinging to the one-armed embrace of a bearish man in a blue cap. Then the door fell shut behind us; the raw after-rain air was biting against my lungs; McCauley was peering up and down the street. Suddenly, he set off for the harbour at a brisk pace. I followed in pursuit, my hands lodged deeply in my pockets, my limbs tensed against the chill of the night. Shortly I could no longer tell if the numbness I felt was due to the rum or merely the cold.

There is a sharp declivity in the street as it falls away to the shoreline and as I came across it, trailing McCauley by several yards, I perceived the harbour spread out before us, the sea still choppy from the storm, several of the taller masts sail-less and rocking dimly against the clouded sky. The ships were creaking at their moorings and here and there, few and far between, lone shipboard lanterns burned brokenly, keeping the nightwatch. And further ahead of us, already out on the quays, I could see another figure which I took to be the sailor, Barry, moving forward unsteadily in a drunken stagger-walk. He was within hailing distance because I could already hear fragments of a song he was singing and shouting to himself as it carried back to us, and I couldn't understand why McCauley didn't call out to him.

Just before the paving of the street gave way to the wood of the dock, to the left, lay the crumbling remains of an ancient sea wall. There, McCauley paused for a moment, kneeling down as I came abreast of him. When he stood he held in one hand what I took to be a broken chunk of masonry. He turned and spoke, his face expressionless in shadow, but the voice was expressive enough, festering with the heat of an unresolved fever. He spat the words out at me, somehow both sibilant and guttural at the same time.

"Get yourself a rock, boy!"

Abruptly he turned away again and I saw that what I had taken for masonry was heavier in his hand, an old brick with a sharp protrusion on one side. His words of earlier came back to me—"We'll take one down, tonight!"—and at once, in a wave of nausea, I understood what we were about. The rum turned sour and cold in my belly and next I found myself holding a nearby piling, retching stale phlegm into the pitching harbour water just like McCauley. No, Barry was no forger, just an accursed "gay boy" we were going to roll, outwardly for the papers he possessed, but in truth more to consumate my companion's evening than for anything else.

McCauley was ahead of me again, about fifty yards behind Barry, moving in a half-crouch with the brick raised as if he were going to strike any moment—while the sailor staggered on unawares, muttering his song. Without question, I knew that I had to prevent what was about to transpire. I fought down the sickness and moving into a crouch myself, running, I quickly closed the distance between myself and McCauley. With one hand I grasped the wrist of his raised arm, with the other I encircled his chest. He turned in my hold with a strength and quickness I had not expected, our legs became entangled and we fell together, striking dully against the dampened wood of the pier. My hands grappled for control and he writhed beneath me. Amidst the sounds of our suddenly heavy breathing I looked down into his face, close by mine. With the realization of what was happening his eyes burned with righteous anger and fury, and I saw that in that moment I had now become the object of his passion.

As I lost his wrist the brick ascended rapidly in a flailing arc to strike the side of my skull and fly skidding across the deck, into the water. A wave of blood red swept before my eyes, blanketing out the twisted image beneath me, and I had to fight for consciousness. Yet as my sight cleared, I was the one now seized by a fury and passion compete! All my abhorrence of the man rose up within me far more sickening than the soured rum. Beyond control, my hands searched out the speckled flesh of his throat, the worn cords of his neck, and locked set upon their course as surely as the grip of madness had locked itself upon me. Even as a part of my mind began to clear, I could see that there was no way to stop. I was split, my consciousness remote, small and helpless, returning only in bits and snatches, yet watching it all. Watching as the life drained from all of it, the gnarled hands which beat more and more feebly against my chest, the sweat that stippled his brow as finely as in the Bathysphere because it was the life-fear which had given birth to them both, the tongue which would never stop wagging its nonsense now pushing through his blanched lips and soon to wag no more, his progeric wrinkles which would grow no more, his petty passions, his petty knowledge and lies and foolery, all of it, moribund, moribund, faltering . . . . still.

He lay beneath me, as wretched in death as he had been in life. A hoarse animal sobbing wrenched itself from my throat as the rage left me empty.

· · · ·

It is dawn now and at last I am at sea, the last recruit of a dilapidated freighter not much better than a shanghai ship. A fading, nacreous moon bobs amidst the rigging. Behind me the harbour is cast in dull chiaroscuro—sky off-white, water grey, the buildings of the city spread in dark clumpings which thin to a black filigree before falling beneath the horizon. Then there is nothing but the capacious and motile sea, my sea of freedom, and with the full morning sun the waves and wavelets sparkle, a thousand eidolons of light spin dancing across the waters. But that sea is below the bow, beyond my reach, and it is only its derivative, the salt spray, which cools my cheeks and washes the swollen cut which mars my temple. Yes, McCauley has left his mark upon me, and no doubt it will heal to a worthy and lasting scar. Yet by now *I* am already known as "McCauley." I have my identification papers, both ticket of passage and *momento mori,* and although they say that I am older than I look, that my perfect right knee is trick and my grey eyes blue, they have proven sufficient upon this garbage scow. They do not really care about papers here: the most awkward forgery would pass. McCauley's explication of the "necessary" papers was just more of his nonsense or mendacity—it no longer matters which.

In any case, I have found my ship and my berth, and although the deck may be grease-slickened, the crew unsavory, and its passage slow, it will doubtless carry me to my appropriate destination. I am a sailor, locked within the wave roar and water roll. I am a sailor truly, my body laced with tattoos of my own making—it makes no difference that I am the only one who can see them. The woods are behind me. Lily is behind me. McCauley is behind me. All, behind me and with me. The weight of my history hangs in the gallows of my chest and there is no way to cut it down.

Contributors Notes

Bart Alberti came through the Berkeley Poets' Workshop in the early 1970's. **Chris Bahr** helped edit *Anonymous, A Journal for the Woman Writer.* She received her M.A. in creative writing from San Francisco State. **Dan Balderston** was active in the Berkeley Poets' Workshop in the early 1970's. **Madeline T. Bass** lives in New Jersey, where she works with Poetry in the Schools. She is the author of two books of poems, *Keeping House in the Forest* (Farleigh Dickinson, 1977) and *Electric Blanket,* which will soon be published in England. **Belden** is a college teacher and psychotherapist. He lives in Berkeley and is the author of *Snake Blossoms* (BPW&P, 1977). **Ramsay Bell** lives in Berkeley. She is currently a student at the San Francisco Art Institute. **Paul Bendix** graduated from the San Francisco State writing program in the mid-1970's. **Bruce Boston** lives in Oakland and teaches creative writing at John F. Kennedy University. He is a recipient of the Pushcart Prize for fiction, and author of the collection of stories, *Jackbird* (BPW&P, 1976). **Karen Brodine** lives in San Francisco and works as a typesetter. She is the author of several books of poems, most recently *Illegal Assembly* (Hanging Loose, 1980). **Dorothy Bryant** is a native San Franciscan. Her novels include *The Kin of Ata Are Waiting for You, Miss Giardino,* and *The Garden of Eros.* She now lives in Berkeley where she and her husband publish Ata Books. **John Allen Cann** was active in the Berkeley Poets' Co-op in the mid-1970's. He now lives in Southern California. **Betty Coon** lives in Berkeley and teaches at Diablo Valley College. She is the author of *Seaward* (BPW&P, 1978). **Michael Covino** lives in Berkeley. His stories and poems have appeared in a number of magazines, including *Chelsea,* the *Chicago Review,* and *Kayak.* His film reviews have been published in *Film Quarterly.* **Peri Danton** lives in Berkeley. **Lucille Day** has published in *California Living, San Francisco Review of Books,* and *The Hudson Review.* She recently completed her Ph.D. in science education at the University of California, Berkeley. **Patricia Dienstfrey** was born in Montreal, Canada, and grew up in New England. She lives in Berkeley with her husband and three children, and works as a typesetter for a local newspaper. She is also a book printer and editor with Kelsey St. Press. **Mario Donatelli** was born in New York. He is the author of *Songbook,* and currently attends the University of California, Berkeley. **Kit Duane** lives in Berkeley. She is the author of the children's book *A Girl Named Hero,* and is active with Kelsey St. Press. **Greg Dunn** was a member of the Berkeley Poets' Co-op in the early 1970's. **Quinton Duval** received his M.A. in creative writing from the University of Montana. He is the author of *Guerilla Letters* (Quarterly West) and a regular contributor to *Artweek.* **Charles Entrekin,** a founding member of the Berkeley Poets' Co-op, holds an M.F.A. in creative writing and is the author of two books of stories and poems, *All Pieces of a Legacy* (BPW&P, 1975) and *Casting for the Cutthroat* (Thunder City, 1978). He is the Associate Director of the Center for Contemporary Writing at John F. Kennedy University, Orinda. **Marcia Falk** received her Ph.D. in English from Stanford University. Her poetry has appeared in many anthologies, and her translation of *The Song of Songs* (HBJ) was published in 1978. She is currently teaching at the State University of New York, Binghamton. **Ted Fleischman** received his M.A. in physics from the University of Chicago. Since moving to California, he has taught high school math and worked in various technical fields, including spectroscopy and fusion electronics. He is the author of *Half a Bottle of Catsup* (BPW&P, 1978). **Stewart Florsheim** is a technical writer, and lecturer in creative writing at John F. Kennedy University. He lives in San Francisco. **Alice Fulton** lives in New York, where she is a member of the Writers' Community Workshop. **John Gardner** lives in Alameda. **Gus Gustafson** lives in Berkeley and teaches at Diablo Valley College. **Bruce Hawkins** lives in Berkeley and sells poetry magazines on the street. He is the author of *Wordrows* (BPW&P, 1975). **Michael Helm** is the editor/publisher of *City Miner* magazine. His most recent book of poems is *Snap Thoughts* (1979). **M.L. Hester** lives in Greensboro, North Carolina, and has published in over a hundred literary magazines, including the *Mississippi Review* and *Southern Poetry Review*. **Susan Hoffman** is the director of the People's Theatre Coalition in San Francisco. **Peter Holland** lives in San Francisco and teaches physics at City College. He edits and publishes the magazine, *Galleryworks*. **Burghild Holzer** is from Austria. She teaches creative writing at San Francisco State. **Bruce Horovitz** is a graduate of Colorado State University. He has worked as a journalist and his articles and poems have appeared in numerous magazines. **Betsy Gladstone Huebner** is a painter of the Northwest Passage and coastal areas from Pt. Reyes to beyond the Aleutian Chain. She lives in Berkeley. **Nick Johnson** did graduate work and taught creative writing at Catholic University, New York. He is currently teaching in the New York Program of the New College of California. **Hilda Johnston** was born in New York. She is a long-time resident of Berkeley and teaches at Laney College. **Carla Kandinsky** is active in the Berkeley Women's Center writing workshops. She has published in many magazines and is currently collaborating on a book concerning Berkeley. **Sarah Kirsch** has published three books of poetry and is also a widely published translator. She moved from East to West Germany in 1977 after cultural disputes with the East German government. She lives in West Berlin with her son. **Charles Klein** attended the Berkeley Poets' Workshop in the mid-1970's and more recently has become a songwriter and performer. **Phyllis Koestenbaum** teaches creative writing at San Francisco State. Her work has appeared in a number of magazines, including *Nimrod* and *Contemporary California Women Poets*. **John Krich** is the author of *Bump City* (City Miner Books, 1979) and *Chicago Is*. His fiction has appeared in *Commentary* and other magazines. He lives in Oakland. **David Lampert** lived in Boston for most of his life, and for the last few years has resided in the Bay Area. He is the author of one book of poems, *The Wind in the Fire,* and is currently working as a computer analyst. **Mary Lane** lives in Chicago, where she writes about current events for an encyclopedia supplement. Her poems have appeared in *Pushcart Prize II, Interstate,* and a number of other publications. **Marina LaPalma** is completing a degree in poetry and recording media at Mills College. She is one of the editors of Kelsey St. Press and co-producer of the weekly KPFA radio program, "Focus on Women in Music." Her poems have appeared in many magazines and anthologies. **Lyn Lifshin** lives in New York. Her recent books include *Plymouth Woman, Tangled Vines,* and *Offered By Owner,* a book and record set. **Anthony Manousos** teaches at Cook College, Rutgers. His poems have appeared in many magazines, and he is a contributor to *20th Century Science Fiction Writers* (St. Martin's Press). **Richard Marcus** participated in the Berkeley Poets' Workshop in 1976, then moved to Northern California. **Edward Martinez** is a recent contributor. **Clive Matson** grew up on an avocado ranch in San Diego County. He now lives in Oakland, where he operates a letterpress and teaches poetry workshops. He is the author of four books of poetry, including the forthcoming *On the Inside* (Thorpe Springs Press). **Linda McCloud** received her M.A. from San Francisco State. She now lives in Washington, D.C. and teaches at American University. **Milo Miles** has an M.A. from the University of Montana. **Laura Moriarty** lives in San Francisco and is the author of *2 Cross Seizings* (Sombre Reptiles, 1980). **Rachel Nahem** is a Bay Area resident and graduate of San Francisco State. **Peter Najarian** is the author of the novel *Voyages* (Pantheon, 1971) and the narrative *Wash Me On Home, Mama* (BPW&P, 1978). He is currently teaching at Scripps College, Pomona. **Alicia Ostriker's** latest book of poems is *A Dream of Springtime* (Smith Horizon Press). Her poems and articles have appeared widely in such publications as *Esquire* and *American Poetry Review.* She teaches at Rutgers University. **Frank Polite** is the author of *Letters of Transit* (City Miner Books, 1979). He lives with his son in Youngstown, Ohio. **Aaron Poller** was born in New York City. He received his B.A. in English from the University of Pennsylvania. He lives with his wife and daughter in Landsdale, Pennsylvania, where he works as a psychiatric technician. **Kathleen Raven** was active in the Berkeley Poets' Co-op in the early 1970's. **Nina Rogozen** lives in Seattle with her daughter and husband. **Ed Saucier** is from Texas and came through the Berkeley Poets' Workshop in 1976. **Laura Schiff** is a writer and translator, currently translating novels from Hungarian and Romanian. **Roswell Spafford** teaches creative writing at San Francisco State, and is currently working on a novel about the late Sixties. **Rona Spalten's** stories have appeared in a number of magazines and anthologies, including *New Worlds* and *Fiction.* She received her M.A. from Sonoma State College and is currently living in Sebastopol, California, where she is working on a novel. **Adriano Spatola** was born in Yugoslavia. Since 1971, he has lived near Parma, Italy, where he edits the magazine *Tam-Tam.* He is the author of several books of poetry, available in translation from Red Hill Press. **Jennifer Stone** was born in Arizona. She received her M.A. in creative writing from San Francisco State. Her stories have appeared in a number of publications, including *City Miner, Plexus* and *Mother Jones,* and she is the author of *Over by the Caves* (BPW&P, 1977). **Judith Stone** has a degree in comparative religions from U.C. Berkeley. **Richard Strong** is an agricultural consultant and freelance writer. He is building his own home in Orinda, California. **Susan Strong** teaches at the University of California, Berkeley, in the Rhetoric Department. She has published poetry in a number of magazines. **Laurel Taylor** received her degree in creative writing from Mills College. She is living on a barge in Holland. **Margaret Teague** attended the Berkeley Poets' Workshop in 1974, 1975. **Jim Tinen** was active in the Berkeley Poets' Co-op in the mid-1970's. **Rod Tulloss** is one of the founding members of both the Berkeley Poets' Co-op and the U.S. 1 Poets' Co-op in Princeton. He is the author of *December Fishing* (1978) and his articles and poems have appeared in a variety of magazines, including *American Poetry Review, Small Press Review* and *Black Box.* He lives with his wife in Roosevelt, New Jersey. **JoAnn Ugolini** is an artist and writer and lives in Berkeley. **Paul Vangelisti** lives in Los Angeles where he works for KPFK and is the co-editor of Red Hill Press. His books include *The Extravagant Room* and *Portfolio.* **Dorothy Wall** has an M.A. in creative writing from San Francisco State, and teaches with Vista College. She lives in Oakland with her daughter. **Sharon Williams** lives in Berkeley. In addition to writing she works in photography and silkscreen. **Ann Woolfolk** was born in New Orleans. She has studied art in Argentina, Chile, Louisiana and New Jersey, where she is currently living. She has four children and works as a freelance art critic and illustrator. **Richard Wyatt** passed through the Berkeley Poets' Workshop in the early 1970's. He was on his way to India. **John Yurechko** was born in Pennsylvania, currently lives in Oakland. His main interest is history, and he is currently writing a book on psychological warfare. **William Zander** has published in *Kayak, Poetry Northwest* and other magazines. He is the author of *Distances* (Solo Press).

Key

Number after authors' names indicates page on which their work begins in the anthology. Following titles of individual works, the numbers or titles in parentheses indicate the Co-op volume or chapbook in which they first appeared.